By Donald G. Bloesch

Centers of Christian Renewal
The Christian Life and Salvation
The Crisis of Piety
The Christian Witness in a Secular Age
Christian Spirituality East and West (coauthor)
The Reform of the Church
The Ground of Certainty
Servants of Christ (editor)
The Evangelical Renaissance
Wellsprings of Renewal
Light a Fire
The Invaded Church
Jesus Is Victor!: Karl Barth's Doctrine of Salvation
The Orthodox Evangelicals (coeditor, with Robert E. Webber)
Essentials of Evangelical Theology, Vol. I: God, Authority, and Salvation
Essentials of Evangelical Theology, Vol. II: Life, Ministry, and Hope
The Struggle of Prayer
Faith and Its Counterfeits

Is the Bible Sexist?

Beyond Feminism and Patriarchalism

DONALD G. BLOESCH

CROSSWAY BOOKS • WESTCHESTER, ILLINOIS
A DIVISION OF GOOD NEWS PUBLISHERS

 Published by Crossway Books, a division of Good News Publishers, Westchester, Illinois 60153.

First printing, 1982.

Printed in the United States of America.

Library of Congress Catalog Card Number 81-71344
ISBN 0-89107-243-8

To Rudolf Schade,
my former teacher at Elmhurst
College, in appreciation of his
friendship and encouragement
through the years.

Contents

Foreword

This book has been written partly to counter the growing demands of feminists to revise the language about God in Scripture and in the liturgy of the church. I speak as one who is sympathetic to the feminist concern to do away with blatantly sexist language, but the problem lies in whether the language of Scripture can be revised without sacrificing its meaning. In wrestling with this matter, I have found it necessary to reexamine the whole relationship between men and women—in society and in the church.

After considerable investigation, I have come to the conclusion that there is a biblical alternative to both feminism and patriarchalism. Though the biblical revelation comes to us in the imagery of patriarchalism, this imagery has been drastically altered by the meaning of the Word of God. Biblical faith poses a challenge to both feminism and patriarchalism, but it does not oppose the legitimate concerns and values of either ideology.

The exploitation and oppression of women in our society is indeed to be deplored. Nowhere is this oppression so obvious as in the pornographic magazines and movies which demean and degrade the personhood of woman. The women's liberation movement signifies a necessary and valiant protest against this kind of male chauvinism. I identify myself completely with the demand for equal pay and work opportunities for women as well as respect for the dignity of woman. Yet I have grave reservations about aligning the faith with the ideology of feminism, which seeks to forge a new life- and world-view that at many points stands at variance with the biblical vision of God and the world.

Modern feminism, at least in its dominant strand, signifies a reversion to a monistic world outlook, particularly as this appears in the form of nature mysticism. A fascination with panentheism and pantheism is prominent, reflecting the growing reservations that many feminists have with traditional theism, in which, so it seems, God is separated from the world. The feminist protest is directed not merely against discriminatory employment practices and sexist language, but also against a hierarchical and dualistic understanding of the world and humanity. In place of God the Almighty we are presented with a Mother Goddess or female goddesses who function as symbols of the creative force within nature. Feminists such as Naomi Goldenberg (in her *Changing of the Gods,* Beacon Press, 1979) accept modern witchcraft as the emerging religion of women because it allows them to celebrate the divinity within them. Not all feminists, of course, go this far, but nonetheless an immanental conception of deity is clearly favored over the traditional emphasis on God as transcendent and all-powerful.

As this controversy grows in the church today, it can be shown that both sides stand opposed to male chauvinism and sexism (though I am not including some on the ideological right who refuse to enter into the dialogue). Both sides support women's rights to equal pay and work opportunities. The conflict revolves about women in positions of spiritual leadership and the modification of the language about God. I intend to speak to both these issues in this book.

When I refer to feminism, I have in mind ideological

feminism, including both radical and moderate strands. These two groups share similar goals, and their understanding of life and the world converges at many points; yet they differ on how to attain these goals. I acknowledge a biblical feminism that stands in tension with the modern ideology of feminism, and my own position would be very close to the former. At the same time, because many who call themselves Christian feminists and even evangelical feminists basically share the vision of feminist ideology, I have been led to describe my own position in other terms, though I accept the label of a qualified or biblical feminist.

When I speak of patriarchalism, I am thinking of a cultural ideology that has its roots in the ancient world and that has held sway in most civilizations through the centuries, including the nations of the West until very recent times. It is valid to distinguish between various types of patriarchalism, but even a so-called Christian patriarchalism stands at variance with the biblical perspective on male-female relationships. Nevertheless, I could accept the label of a biblically qualified patriarchalist, though I am not wholly comfortable with it.

It is my contention that the biblical view signifies the nullification and transcendence of both feminism and patriarchalism. While seeking to build bridges between those who hold to the opposing positions, I also try to point them toward an alternative that calls into question their ideological commitments. *Ideology* in the context of this study signifies an integral idea system that serves to justify the social needs and aspirations of a particular interest-group or class. My position is that biblical faith cannot be reconciled or harmonized with any cultural ideology, though it can learn from the truth as well as the error in every ideology. Indeed, as I shall try to show, ideological feminism and biblical faith represent two different religions. Similarly, biblical faith must not be confused with the semi-tribal patriarchalism now in vogue with the recrudescence of the ideological right, where personal integrity is sacrificed to family or clan loyalty and "the total woman" becomes the total doormat instead of the helpmate and partner of man.

In this book I speak as a man who is *for* woman. I regret that I have not always been as active as I should have been in defending the legitimate rights of women and in decrying sexism, the sin of treating women as inferiors. In this, I share in the guilt of most men today. Yet I must raise my voice in protest against certain excesses in modern feminism which I regard as undermining women as well as the moral fabric of our society.

As I see it, both patriarchalism and feminism result in the oppression and isolation of woman. In traditional patriarchal culture, it was the wife's business to make her husband successful, not the husband's business to make his wife happy. Subordination has generally meant in these circles abject submission to the dictates of the will of the man. The woman may be permitted to be a teacher of other women, but never of men. In modern feminist ideology, it is the wife's prerogative to fulfill herself, even at the expense of her obligations to her husband and family. Whether married or unmarried, the woman is encouraged to pursue a goal in which she realizes autonomy or independence. Both feminism and patriarchalism accentuate loneliness in the existence of woman, and the alternative that I propose is designed to overcome this.

The authority in this study is Holy Scripture. I refuse to discard those parts of Scripture that do not agree with any preconceptions that I might entertain. I do not subscribe to a canon within the canon in the sense that only certain books of the Bible are normative for me. On the other hand, I accept the principle of levels of revelation, contending that the Old Testament must be interpreted in the light of the New. Instead of a canon within the canon, I would rather speak of a center and a periphery of the canon, of peaks and plains within the canon. Because I believe that all Scripture is inspired by the Spirit of God, I uphold an underlying theological unity in Scripture within and behind the obvious theological and cultural diversity.

Against those who appeal to current philosophy or to the latest findings in the social sciences in order to determine what is valid in Scripture, I contend that Scripture can only be interpreted in its own light. There is a grave risk in trying to separate the transcendental or existential meaning of Scripture from its culturally and historically conditioned form. We have the treasure of the Word of God only in the earthen vessel of the language of Zion (the mythopoetic imagery of Scripture), and we hear this Word precisely in its historical concreteness and specificity. To seek for a Word beyond the prophetic and apostolic witness is as dangerous as seeking for a God beyond his self-revelation and incarnation in the historical Jesus Christ. This does not mean that we cannot differentiate between what is culturally contingent and what is of abiding significance in Scripture. It does mean that the criterion for judging the relative value of the various parts of Scripture must come from Scripture itself and not from contemporary secular wisdom.

The Bible witnesses neither to a patriarchal nor a feminist ideology, but to the grace of God which breaks through all ideological barriers and thereby makes possible reconciliation between people in warring camps. The ideological polarization today on the issue of women's liberation can be resolved only by a fresh reappropriation of the abiding insights of Holy Scripture as they are brought home to us by the illumination of the Holy Spirit.

Acknowledgments

I wish to acknowledge the substantial help that I have received in this work from Dr. Arthur Cochrane of Wartburg Theological Seminary, Dr. Joseph Mihelic of the University of Dubuque Theological Seminary, and Fathers Benedict Ashley, Benedict Viviano, and Ralph Powell of the Aquinas Institute of Theology. My indebtedness to the writings of Dr. Karl Barth will become readily apparent to the reader.

Many thanks are due to my wife Brenda for her insightful criticisms and her painstaking work as a copy editor of this book. I also wish to thank Miss Lillian Staiger and Mrs. Edith Baule, members of our seminary library staff, for their immense aid in helping me locate needed references. In addition, I am deeply grateful to Mrs. Peg Saunders for her careful typing of the final manuscript.

Scripture citations are from the *Revised Standard Version* unless otherwise indicated. The abbreviations are: NEB for *The New English Bible,* NIV for *The New International Version,* and KJV for the King James Version.

In this unheard of process, by which woman assumes so decisive and transcendent a meaning for man, it is confirmed that it was not good for man to be alone; that he really needed a helpmeet, and that without the existence of this helpmeet his own creation would really not have been complete.

Karl Barth

What if . . . the sweeping, doctrinaire egalitarianism of our culture, which makes the concept of "the place of woman" seem either laughable or boorish, and makes that of "subordination" seem insulting, should turn out really . . . to be demonic, uncharitable, destructive of personality, disrespectful of creation and unworkable?

John Howard Yoder

1 / The Present Controversy

A contemporary issue which is creating division within the churches is that of feminism versus patriarchalism. Some theologians—for example, Mary Daly,[1] Helen Luke,[2] and Thomas Parker[3]—have supported the androgynous ideal in which the polarity between masculinity and femininity is transcended. In this perspective, sexual distinctions are downplayed, and unisex becomes the new goal. It is said that people should see themselves as composed of both masculine and feminine elements and should try to integrate these within themselves. Not all feminists adhere to the androgynous ideal, but they generally seek to overcome the masculine-feminine polarity.[4]

Feminism, which appears to be riding the crest of the future, has not been without its critics. Theologians such as Thomas Howard and Dale Vree affirm that masculinity and femininity are ontological distinctions, and that the boundaries between them must be respected. Karl Barth, who espouses a definitely qualified patriarchalism, maintains that "woman must always and in all circumstances be woman; that she must feel and conduct herself as such and not as a man; that the command of the Lord, which is for all eternity, directs both man and woman to their own proper sacred place and forbids all attempts to violate this order."[5] A view that appears to be in accord with historic Christian patriarchy is reflected in Elisabeth Elliot: "God created male and female, the male to call forth, to lead, initiate and rule, and the female to respond, follow, adapt, submit."[6]

The conflict between traditionalism and feminism concerns not only man-woman relations, but also life- and world-views. It even revolves on how God is ultimately conceived and worshiped. Feminists generally seek to revise the language about God to make it more inclusive. God, it is said, should no longer be thought of in exclusively masculine terms. Instead of "God as Father" we should now address God as "Father-Mother" or "heavenly Parent."[7] Some radical feminists, such as Mary Daly and Matthew Fox, seek to transcend personal categories altogether in speaking about God; God now becomes "the ground of being" or "creativity" or "the life force." An official study group in the United Presbyterian Church U.S.A. suggests that we "avoid personal metaphors" for God and instead employ terms "like Rock, Fire, First and the Last, the Holy One, the Eternal One, and Spirit."[8] Those feminists who lean toward monistic mysticism regard God as "the Primal Source," beyond the ethical distinctions of good and evil. Others who are attracted to process philosophy and theology depict God simply as "brother" and "sister" instead of Almighty Father, thereby suggesting that God must struggle as we do toward deeper fulfillment and integration.

Feminists also wish to reconceive the role of the family as being directed to mutual fulfillment rather than the furthering of the husband's career or the raising of children. The "democratic family" is presented as an alternative to the "autocratic family" with its patriarchal authority.[9] In the former, decisions are arrived at by group consensus, and this includes the wishes of the children as well as of the wife.

The meaning of the ministry is also being debated.

Feminists quite naturally press for the ordination of women to the ministry or priesthood, whereas patriarchalists tend to resist such efforts. For the patriarchalist, women may have subordinate roles of service, such as deaconess, but they cannot have apostolic authority to preside at the sacraments, because Scripture reserves this office only for males.

Authority in the feminist perspective is rooted primarily in human experience, particularly feminine experience, not in Scripture.[10] The social sciences are considered to have almost as much authority as the sacred tradition, if not equal or superior authority. It is not uncommon to hear feminists, including evangelical feminists, contend that Paul was "wrong" in his attitude toward women.[11] Sister Ann Patrick Ware, former associate director of the Commission on Faith and Order of the National Council of Churches, goes so far as to suggest that the Word of God "is in need of correction," since it has been "corrupted by the mores of the culture in which it was received."[12]

The meaning of *salvation* is also altered in this perspective. It is reconceived to connote liberation from male oppression or from the patriarchal tradition. It is the discovery and celebration of womanhood. It is the fulfillment and realization of human potential or feminine potential. Jesus Christ becomes only a great prophet with enlightened views on human relations or a pioneer in feminism.

For some feminists, salvation lies in the realization of the androgynous ideal where femininity and masculinity are combined and thereby transcended.[13] Sheila Collins declares that "salvation is that discovery and celebration of the 'other' in ourselves. When men discover their femininity and women their masculinity, then perhaps we can form a truly liberating and mutually enriching partnership."[14] Matthew Fox cites with approval the pseudepigraphal Gospel of Thomas: "Until you make the male female and the female male, you will not enter the kingdom."[15]

It is not surprising that radical feminists tend to support the gay liberation movement, since they completely sever sex from its reproductive or generative purpose. They also propose the "total elimination of sex roles," and this includes a tolerance of lesbian as well as male homosexual relationships. For Mary Daly, in a nonsexist society homosexuals would be free to relate meaningfully and authentically to one another.[16]

Part of the problem is that equality is understood differently by the two sides in this controversy. For feminists, equality means virtual identity so that there are no longer particular roles for women to fulfill, and the same is true for men. For enlightened patriarchalists, men and women are equal in regard to their moral worth before God, but not in the sense of having the very same gifts and abilities. Equality must not be confused with equivalency. Karl Barth sees man and woman as complementary; they are intended by God to supplement one another, not to usurp each other's roles.

Class divisions are prominent in this controversy. The feminist movement draws its principal source of inspiration from the upper middle class, particularly the managerial-professional class. In the lower middle class and poorer classes, even where mothers are working, the desire is that the fathers assume more responsibility in providing for the home and in directing the family. Whereas nearly all feminists are pro-choice on the issue of abortion because of their belief that women should have absolute control over their own bodies, lower middle class and poorer class women tend to be on the antiabortion side.[17]

Feminists who loudly decry the sin of sexism are often guilty of the sin of classism, since they are prone to regard men and women from the lower middle class and poorer classes as "unenlightened." Groups like the Salvation Army and the Church of the Nazarene, which accept and encourage the ordination of women to the ministry, are an embarrassment to feminists in the mainline denominations because those evangelical women teach submission and obedience to authority.

Not all the opposition to feminism has come from those who enthrone the values of the cultural tradition. A Roman Catholic historian of religion, R. C. Zaehner, complains that what has resulted is unisex: "No more males, no more females, and, given the irreversible progress of medical science, maybe no more young and no more old."[18] Erich Fromm declares that the emancipation of women has not meant the emergence of the holy mother who selflessly sacrifices herself for her child; it "did not mean . . . that [woman] was free to develop her specific, as yet unknown, traits and potentialities; on the contrary, she was being emancipated in order to become a bourgeois man."[19] Some critics in the area of the social sciences are lamenting that the women's movement has promoted the confusion of male-female roles and ipso facto has contributed to the increase of "effeminate" men and "masculine" women.[20] Despite his outspoken advocacy of women's rights, Kristar Stendahl acknowledges that the ideology of the feminist movement has its roots "in the Enlightenment or in Hellas or in the cult of Baal," not in the Bible.[21] David Bakan cautions that modern society is in danger of losing sight of the abiding values in patriarchy, particularly those relating to the fatherly responsibility for children.[22]

It should be recognized that within the Christian church both parties in this conflict affirm women's rights in the sense of equality before the law. The enlightened patriarchalist as much as the feminist protests against the shameless exploitation of women in our society and the discrimination against women in the various professions.

Patriarchalists wish to maintain what they believe is a radical contrast between male and female, one that is written into the order of creation and is discernible particularly in the area of spiritual authority.[23] Feminists, on the other hand, tend to deny any legitimacy for the sharp distinction in roles that has characterized the sexes in the past, and particularly as this distinction has governed the life of the family and of the church.

Patriarchalists are accustomed to speaking of the husband as the shield and protector of the wife; though this clearly has biblical support, they often interpret it in such a way that the wife is relegated to the status of a charge and therefore cannot be a genuine helpmate. The wife's obligation is to be entirely at the disposal of her husband, but this tends to curtail or even cancel her responsibilities beyond the family, even where the service of the kingdom is involved.

It is my thesis that neither feminism nor patriarchalism, as traditionally conceived, does justice to the deepest insights of the biblical revelation. Both have a decidedly anthropocentric rather than theocentric orientation: that is to say, both are oriented around the fulfillment of the self rather than service in the kingdom of God. In the case of patriarchalism, the accent is on the success of the husband in his career and on ensuring the continuity of his family name. In the case of feminism, the emphasis is on the fulfillment of personhood, even if this means freedom from traditional roles that stereotype both men and women.

In this discussion I acknowledge the solid contribution of Karl Barth, whose work on the subject of man-woman relationships is of inestimable value. If Barth can be regarded as a patriarchalist, he is so only in a decidedly modified form. In my judgment, Barth transcends the polarity between patriarchalism and feminism, though this is not always clear in his exposition. He is certainly not a male chauvinist, but neither can he be regarded as a feminist, let alone a radical feminist. While affirming the principle of subordination in male-female relations, he qualifies it in the light of the biblical witness.[24] As will be seen, I go further than Barth in the area of God-language in that I am willing to consider modifications in the traditional nomenclature concerning God, though my approach will not meet the expectations of most feminists, including many evangelical feminists.

Like Barth, Reinhold Niebuhr was also sympathetic to the aspirations of women to better themselves in a male-dominated society. Niebuhr, much more than Barth, saw the vocation of women tied to family and motherhood; but he was nevertheless critical of an autocratic patriarchalism that suppressed the legitimate hopes and needs of women:

> A rationalistic feminism is undoubtedly inclined to transgress inexorable bounds set by nature. On the other hand, any premature fixation of certain historical standards in regard to the family will inevitably tend to reinforce male arrogance and to retard justified efforts on the part of the female to achieve such freedom as is not incompatible with the primary function of motherhood.[25]

Those who identify with the cause of woman's liberation are boldly challenging the traditional assumption of patriarchy that the woman's role is to be restricted to children, church, and kitchen. The protest against this particular pattern of male oppression can be shown to have biblical support.[26] At the same time, the Bible must not be used to give religious sanction to a particular ideological bias; instead, it must be the infallible criterion by which we judge all ideologies, including patriarchalism and feminism.

With the rise of modern feminism, we have lost sight of the biblical truth that the vocation of woman is to humanize the man, not to gain mastery over him or to compete with him. Yet woman, as well as man, should be free to pursue the direction in life to which God calls her, even if this means a career outside the family or foregoing marriage. Nonetheless, this career or task in life must not entail contempt or indifference towards the opposite sex. The result can only be the warping or constricting of personality and ipso facto the diminishing of humanity.

A career, like the family, must always be seen as a means to a higher end—the service of the glory of God through ministry to the needs of an ailing and despairing humanity. We find our humanity only by losing ourselves in the service of the welfare of our fellow-humanity, who always exists in a twofold form: male and female.

Today the emphasis is on realizing ourselves as persons. But one can be a person only in relationship to another. Moreover, this relationship cannot be fulfilled apart from a Mediator who understands each party better than that party understands itself. This means that the Mediator must be divine as well as human; he must be the representative of God as well as the representative of humanity. As Christians, we recognize Jesus Christ to be this Mediator. True community occurs, as Bonhoeffer astutely perceived, only when men and women are united in Jesus Christ.[27] Community is subverted when we seek direct or immediate relations with one another, for then we are bypassing the One who purifies and transfigures human relationships, who converts possessive or self-regarding love into the sacrificial love of the cross.

2 / The Man-Woman Relationship in the Bible

The nation of Israel reflected the patriarchal society of the ancient Middle East, but at the same time it transcended that society both in practice and in teaching. Genesis 2:18 records that the Lord said: "It is not good for the man to be alone. I will make a helper suitable for him" (NIV). We see here a certain order or procession. Man is created first, and this means that he is given a kind of headship over woman.[1] At the same time, woman is not created to be a slave or "squaw" for man, but instead a partner or helpmate. It is true that in Genesis 3:16 man is depicted as ruling over woman, but this describes the state of fallen humanity rather than the ideal state in which woman is a companion to man.

Patriarchalism was widely pervasive in the culture of both the Old and New Testaments, though as an ideology it did not become part of the moral law of Israel. Moreover, it was radically corrected not only in the teachings of Jesus and Paul, but also in the vision of the Old Testament prophets. A distinction should always be made between the mores and folkways that characterized the historical and cultural context in which the biblical revelation was transmitted and the authentic teaching of the prophets and apostles, which alone is the Word of God, properly speaking.

Yet it would not be honest to claim that the people of

Israel somehow escaped the rigors of patriarchalism, though attempts were often made to humanize and modify the oppressive structures which this system so often engenders. Like the other cultures of that time, ancient Israel regarded prostitution as licit for males but as reprehensible for females.[2] It seems that the principal duty of the wife was to bear children (cf. Gen. 16:1, 2), preferably males to guarantee heirs to the property of the family.[3] Divorce was never possible on a woman's initiative. A man was expected to marry a virgin, but his own virginity did not need to be intact. A daughter was considered less desirable than a son (Lev. 12:1-5), and she could be sold for debt by her father (Exod. 21:7; cf. Neh. 5:5).[4] When a husband preceded his wife in death, his brother or some other male relative assumed responsibility for her.

Yet patriarchalism was mitigated among the Hebrews and sometimes transcended. In Genesis 1:28 and 2:18 woman is seen as the helpmate of man and not his property, as in patriarchy. These passages also imply that just as manhood comprises the *foundation* of human creation, so womanhood signifies its *culmination*—not exactly a tribute to male supremacy.[5] On the subject of parent-child relations, the fifth commandment says that we must *honor* our parents; but it does not say that we are to give our parents unconditional obedience, which is reserved for God alone.[6]

Neither does the Bible support the strict role differentiation espoused by patriarchalists in which the husband works and the wife must stay at home. In Genesis, both the man and the woman are told to fill the earth and subdue it (Gen. 1:28). Both father and mother are exhorted to discipline and instruct their children (Prov. 1:8; Eph. 6:1-4). Children are not the special province of women. In Proverbs 31:10ff. the ideal wife works outside as well as in the home, making garments and selling them to merchants. The woman in the Song of Songs kept vineyards

(1:6) and pastured flocks (1:8). In Acts we read that Lydia was a businesswoman, a seller of purple goods (Acts 16:14), and Priscilla was a tentmaker (Acts 18:2, 3). Both Ananias and his wife Sapphira sold property (Acts 5:1). In Numbers 27 the daughters of Zelophehad could inherit and therefore own property, if there were no sons to inherit it.

At the same time the Bible regards with disdain a career orientation that neglects all other things, and this is true for both men and women. Although women are not confined to the home, they must still fulfill their responsibility to their family (cf. Prov. 31:27, 28). Men, too, are not to neglect home or family (see 1 Tim. 3:4, 12). Paul urges the older women to train the younger women "to love their husbands and children, to be sensible, chaste . . . kind, and submissive to their husbands" (Titus 2:4, 5).

In the tradition of autocratic patriarchalism, the woman is never to be placed in a position of authority over man. But in the Bible we have many instances of women assuming positions of leadership, even spiritual leadership. Jael and perhaps also Delilah resemble Savior-figures who succeed in trapping the enemy (Judg. 5:24-27; 16:4-21). Deborah became one of the judges, and Esther was a queen whose spiritual authority was recognized by her subjects. The wise women of Tekoa (2 Sam. 14:1-20) and of Abel (2 Sam. 20:14-22) gave political as well as spiritual counsel. In the Apocryphal book of Judith, this heroine of Israel delivered her people from the Assyrians through her political sagacity and daring, and she became for a time the acknowledged spiritual leader of her people. While this book is commonly recognized in scholarly circles as didactic fiction, it is nonetheless remarkably revealing of the way in which the Hebrews were willing to uphold women as models of piety as well as of courage and wisdom. The prophet Jeremiah even predicted the overthrow of patriarchy: "For the Lord has created a new thing on the earth: a woman protects a man" (Jer. 31:22). He may here be pointing to the coming of the Messianic age where the woman protects the Christ-child from the dragon (cf. Rev. 12).[7]

Nowhere do we see patriarchalism so radically transcended as in the life and teachings of our Lord. Jesus called the Jewish women "daughters of Abraham" (Luke 13:16), thereby according them a spiritual status equal to that of men. In Luke 8:1-3 and Mark 15:40, 41 we find two different lists of women who are said to be traveling companions of Jesus and his disciples. Here is reflected "a view of women and men liberated from the strong prohibitions which the pious fear of sexual license had long before created."[8] Jesus' relationship to Mary and Martha as well as to Mary Magdalene indicates a man who was sensitive to the feelings and needs of women. His teaching was not reserved for a select male elite, but instead he felt free to instruct women and converse with them on spiritual matters. Jesus sharply challenged conventional wisdom when he asserted that prostitutes would enter the kingdom of heaven before Jewish religious leaders (Matt. 21:31, 32) because they, unlike the latter, accepted the preaching of John the Baptist.

Paul is commonly cited as a defender of a rigid patriarchalism, but this is to misunderstand him.[9] To be sure, Paul declares in 1 Corinthians 11:3, "The head of every man is Christ, the head of a woman is her husband, and the head of Christ is God." Some scholars argue that "head" (*kephale*) in the Pauline epistles generally means "source" or "origin," rather than authority, and this would not indicate basic subordination.[10] Undoubtedly there is a dimension of truth in this position. Yet I agree with Barth that Paul is indicating a relationship of superordination and subordination, as is definitely implied in 1 Corinthians 11:7-9. These concepts, however, are drastically altered so that the headship of the husband is seen as analogous to that of Christ who was exalted in his humiliation.[11] To say that the man is the head of the woman means that he is the protector of the woman. The subjection of the wife to the husband is "as to the Lord" (Eph. 5:22), which is probably not meant to be any stronger than "as it is fitting in the Lord" (Col. 3:18).

In Paul's theology, subordination does not connote inferiority or passivity, but service-in-fellowship. He speaks of subordination in such a way that the emphasis is on mutual adaptation and coordination. The authority to which woman bows in her subordination is not so much that of her husband as that of the order to which both are subject. As Barth puts it: "This subordination of woman is primarily and essentially to the Lord and only secondarily and unessentially to man."[12] Moreover, within the context of the subordination of woman to man there is a mutual subordination (Eph. 5:21) in which the husband willingly sacrifices his own interests and desires for the sake of his wife. The husband is even obliged to give up his life for his wife as Christ gave his life for the church (Eph. 5:25).

The principal difference between "subordination" in the Pauline epistles (and in the Bible generally) and in the patriarchalism of the ancient world is that the former understands this as a free and loving subordination. It is not subservience (as in historical patriarchalism), but loving assistance. Man and woman in themselves are equal, just as are Christ and the Father in the Trinity. Yet, for the accomplishment of the work of redemption Christ and the Holy Spirit voluntarily subordinate themselves to the Father. Similarly, the wife in a Christian household is called to submit herself freely to the will of her husband, so that the family might be kept intact, and even more importantly so that the kingdom of God might be advanced in the world.

This does not mean that the wife must never take issue with her husband, that she cannot correct her husband when he is in error; yet it does imply that his is the dominant voice in determining the means and place of livelihood for the family. Sarah felt free to reproach Abraham (Gen. 16:5); she also took the initiative in directing her husband to take her maid in order to have children by her (Gen. 16:2; cf. 1 Sam. 25; 2 Kings 4:8-10). At the same time, she gave him unswerving support in the way in which he chose to work out his vocation. She even went along with his subterfuge when he introduced her to Abimelech as his sister rather than his wife (Gen. 20). Rebekah also exerted significant influence in her household, going so far as to deceive her husband Isaac in securing a blessing for her son Jacob. She also persuaded Isaac to send Jacob back to Paddan-aram so that he could marry among his own people (Gen. 27, 28). Yet Rebekah, like Sarah, did not seek to determine the manner or place in which Isaac sought to serve the Lord, but followed his leading in this respect. She was a dutiful wife, but not a slave or mere concubine with no mind or will of her own. Within the framework of leading and following, there was mutual respect and mutual correction.

The husband is not to "lord it over" his wife in the manner of the Gentiles (Matt. 20:25, 26). Like Christ, he is to exercise his lordship in the role of a servant. C. S. Lewis in his *Four Loves* speaks of the new crowns won by the husband in marriage. The crown of sex is a paper crown, but the second crown is one of thorns, in which the man becomes lord of his wife by being her servant.[13]

Headship as Paul understood this does not mean domination. Indeed, the husband who becomes a tyrant has abdicated his role in the family. Headship does mean that the husband is responsible for the family in a way in which his wife is not. She, too, has responsibilities, but they are not the very same as those of her husband. The husband is the provider; the wife is the home-builder. But these are not laws that govern the Christian family. Instead, they are guidelines that simply indicate a difference in realizing vocations. Man and woman are not equivalent but complementary. Each supplements the special gifts and capabilities of the other. The Bible disclaims the authoritarian headship of patriarchy, but retains the imagery of headship with its office of initiating authority and of final responsibility and answerability for the family.

Paul's command to the women in 1 Corinthians to keep their heads veiled in worship (11:2-16) is often misconstrued as the fruit of a latent misogyny. On the contrary, Paul was simply focusing on a custom endemic to his Semitic cultural background and using it to remind woman that her vocation is realized in conjunction with that of man, who is designated as her *kephale* (enabler, nourisher) just as she is his helpmate and glory (1 Cor. 11:7). Barth suggests that in the Corinthian church the fellowship was being disturbed by women who were challenging apostolic authority.[14] There can be no fellowship except where a certain order and distinctiveness are observed. But Paul was by no means absolutizing the practice of veiling, as some biblical literalists suppose. He was only indicating that women who were rebelling against this command were denying their womanliness. His purpose may also have been to safeguard their reputations as honorable women and maintain their image as women of God, since common prostitutes who frequented the streets of Corinth never wore the veil.[15] If Paul were living today, he would very probably ask that women in church dress as is fitting for respectable women and not as men, to avoid any confusion in sexes and roles.[16]

Paul's position on man-woman relationships differs radically from the Jewish rabbinic tradition, as well as from the patriarchal Graeco-Roman culture of the time. In rabbinic usage a woman was designated only as the wife of a particular man, whereas Paul in his Epistle to the Romans greeted the women by name. Among the Greeks, men and women did not eat together or even share the same sleeping quarters. Men spent most of their time outside the house, where the wife was confined. Intellectual conversations between husband and wife were discouraged, and many husbands sought out the company of brilliant young men for this purpose. Paul, by contrast, encouraged the wife to ask questions and the husband to discuss spiritual matters with her (1 Cor. 14:35). He pointed out that if one member is deficient, the whole body suffers (1 Cor. 12:24-26). He rejected the segregation of the sexes both in the home and at worship (cf. 1 Cor. 11:11). Moreover, he affirmed the full equality of sexual rights in marriage, insisting that each partner meet the erotic needs of the other (1 Cor. 7:3-5).[17]

The Magna Carta of Christian liberty is Galatians 3:28—"There is neither Jew nor Greek, slave nor free, male nor female, for you are all one in Christ Jesus" (NIV). Paul was insistent that in Christ there is a basic equality, that men and women are equal heirs to salvation. Yet it is impermissible to conclude from this that no members of Christ's body have greater moral excellence than any others, that no one's work in the kingdom has greater spiritual or practical significance than any one else's (though this is not to imply that such things are based on sex). This text must also not be taken to mean that Paul did not acknowledge a differentiation in roles either in society or in the family of the church. Even though he drastically reinterpreted the master-slave relationship so that master and slave were seen as essentially brothers in Christ (when both were believers), he did not for that reason deny the difference in the function of an employer and an employee.[18] The conflict between men and women portrayed in Genesis 3 is done away with in Christ (Eph. 5), but not the hierarchical structure implied in Genesis 2 (though this is now seen in the light of Christ's humiliation and exaltation).

Another area in which patriarchalism is radically altered

in the New Testament is in the respect accorded to celibacy. Celibacy is considered a threat to the integrity of the family in patriarchal societies, because the celibate renounces the task of preserving the family heritage and name.[19] His loyalty is no longer to the clan, but to a higher order of existence—in this case, the kingdom of God. Jesus affirmed that all who do the will of the Father in heaven are his brothers and sisters (Matt. 12:48-50). Both Jesus and Paul embraced celibacy, regarding it as a state not more worthy than marriage but with more practical advantages, since it frees one for full-time, exclusive service to the kingdom (cf. Luke 18:28-30; 1 Cor. 7:8, 9, 25-38).

The relationship between the sexes is clarified by the two orders which are reflected in the Bible—creation and redemption. Man is given the office of headship in creation, but his headship is distorted because of human sin. Whereas in fallen creation the relationship of woman to man is one of servile subordination, this relationship is transformed in the order of redemption to become one of loving, voluntary subordination. In the order of redemption the differences between men and women are no longer an occasion for discord, but now become the means to mutual enrichment. Moreover, the subordination of woman to man is accompanied by the subordination of man to woman, though this is of a different kind. In the order of redemption the wife is more than a helpmate to her husband. She is now a sister in Christ, and this means that she fully participates in the spiritual leadership of the family.

Today there is an attempt to drive a wedge between the cultural expression of the faith as we find it in Scripture and the scriptural witness to Jesus Christ. It is said that the church is bound not to the mythological garment in which the faith is enclosed, but only to the abiding values of the faith. The trouble with this approach is that it loses sight of the fact that we have the divine content only in the cultural form in which it is given to us. For better or worse, we hear the witness to Jesus Christ through the expression and imagery of patriarchy, even though this witness transcends and alters the meaning of the language in which it comes to us.

In this regard, L. S. Thornton urges us to see that

> it is impossible to tear religion out of the external forms in which its inward unity is clothed, or to regard it as a thing-in-itself wholly independent of those forms. . . . The attempt to isolate an essential core of religion from the external forms in which it was originally clothed merely results in an unconscious re-clothing of the supposed core in forms more familiar to the mind of the person who undertakes the hazardous operation.[20]

In Paul's view there is a first and second, an above and below, a before and after (1 Cor. 11:1-16; Eph. 5:21-33). Paul was thinking primarily of the relationship between Christ and his church, and only secondarily of that between husband and wife; but the latter is grounded in the former. The woman becomes a sign of what all Christians should be in relationship to Christ. Mary, the mother of Christ, is the example of ideal womanhood, for she was a handmaiden to the Lord. But all Christians are to be servants of Christ. Indeed, as believers we are all brides of Christ, men as well as women. This is not, however, to deny continuing distinctions between man and woman, husband and wife; to erase these distinctions, as radical feminists wish to do, is to endorse the egalitarian family and the loss of the subordination of children to parents.

The Bible does not preach autocracy either in the parent-child relationship or in the husband-wife relationship. It does teach a certain dependence of the wife on the husband and of the children on their parents, just as the church, as the vessel of the Spirit, is dependent on Christ and Christ is dependent on God. But this dependence does not connote inferiority but instead complementarity, a subordination not in essence (as in patriarchalism) but in function. And because this is a purely modalistic subordination, the Bible allows for occasions in which the woman assumes headship over the man, both spiritual and civil, thereby attesting the essential equality of man and woman before God.

Unlike many of the ancient Greeks and Gnostics, the biblical writers did not uphold an androgynous ideal. The distinction between man and woman is ontological, rooted in the very order of existence. Barth puts it very succinctly: "Humanity was not for them an ideal beyond masculinity and femininity. But masculinity and femininity themselves, in their differentiation and unity, constituted humanity."[21] This distinction between masculine and feminine persists into eternity, for we read that Jesus was raised bodily as a man. Enoch and Elijah were assumed into heaven as men. Elijah and Moses appeared on the Mount of Transfiguration as men. Church tradition has generally pictured the assumption of Mary into heaven as that of a woman, not of an angel. Moreover, her frequent appearances to saints here on earth through the medium of dreams and visions are always in the form of a woman. Such private "revelations" do not have the same authority for faith as the public revelation given in Scripture, but they nonetheless cast light on how the fathers and doctors of the church through the ages have regarded sexual identity in the life hereafter. Eternity does not cancel the distinctions between the sexes, even though sexuality in the narrow sense (i.e., genital sexuality) is transcended in the eternal kingdom of God (cf. Matt. 22:23-33; Luke 20:27-36).

The Bible regards homosexuality with profound disapproval, because it signifies a prideful attempt to deny the biblical claim that woman was given to man as a helpmate.

Man cannot live an authentic existence in the eyes of God apart from woman. Indeed, he can realize the goal for which he was created only in relationship to woman. He is the head of woman, but woman is the glory of man (1 Cor. 11:7).

This is not to imply that all people are called into marriage, but it does mean that even the man who has a celibate vocation can live a Christian life only in cooperation if not in active collaboration with woman.[22] Similarly, the woman who embraces a celibate life can realize her vocation only in conjunction with that of man, and indeed not apart from a certain dependence on man. The radical feminist who sounds the call to total emancipation from dependence on the opposite sex is only fostering a climate conducive to lesbianism.

It should be borne in mind that many of the great saints of the church who embraced a celibate life-style nevertheless cultivated tender and loving relations with members of the opposite sex, though this was the spiritual love that characterizes the kingdom of God, not the carnal love that belongs to the old aeon. This was the case with such renowned ascetics as Francis of Assisi, Francis de Sales, Jeanne Chantal, Teresa of Avila, John of the Cross, Vincent de Paul, and Pascal. Even Augustine, who broke off intimate relations with women upon his conversion, nevertheless maintained a deepening relationship with his mother Monica, whose prayers and counsel played a formative role in his vocation. She was indeed not only his natural mother, but also and even more his spiritual mother.

Just as the Bible cannot furnish support for radical feminism, so it cannot be rightly used to defend any form of sexism. It nowhere sanctions the abuse and exploitation of women. Instead, it emphasizes the need for their care and protection. Some feminists call this condescension, but deference to woman as woman belongs to the very nature of masculinity, just as a certain dependency on the male is of the very essence of femininity.

Although the basic thrust of the Bible is condemnatory of sexism, it must be acknowledged that the culture and times reflected in the Bible were often sexist and blatantly patriarchal. A deepening mistrust of women was apparent in the post-exilic period.[23] In the Apocryphal book of Ecclesiasticus, husbands are advised: "If she does not accept your control, divorce her and send her away" (25:26, NEB). In this same book woman is depicted as the origin of sin, and "it is through her that we all die" (25:24, NEB). Yet on the whole, even in the Old Testament, a woman's status is determined ultimately by her relationship to God. The Bible presents cases of subordination *to* women, both in and out of the family, as well as *by* women.[24]

The tribal patriarchalism of Semitic and Graeco-Roman culture is commonly believed to have intruded into 1 Timothy 2 where Paul (or one of his disciples speaking in his name) issues an injunction forbidding women to speak in public assembly, and exhorting them to dress modestly.[25] He also voices the seemingly patriarchal bias that "woman will be saved through bearing children" (verse 15). First of all, it should be noted that these injunctions are limited to that particular place and time where syncretistic and ascetic movements were decrying marriage and family. Jeremias holds that the emphasis on bearing children is to offset the unnatural abstinence advocated by false teachers.[26]

When the text says that women will be saved through child-bearing, it undoubtedly does not denote the mere act of bearing children, as would be the case in tribal patriarchy. Instead, it means that woman will enjoy the benefits of her salvation in Christ in the vocation of motherhood as opposed to presiding at public assemblies; yet the apostle qualifies this immediately by adding, "if she continues in faith and love and holiness, with modesty." This passage refers not to Eve or to women in general, but only to Christian women who must first of all be mothers in the faith before they are mothers in the flesh. This should remind us that Mary was regarded as a mother in the faith before she became a mother in the flesh (cf. Luke 1:26-38, 46-55; Matt. 12:46-50). The meaning is that women (the wider Pauline context indicates *most* but not *all* women) will find the joy of their salvation in fulfilling their tasks as Christian mothers.

Yet Paul is not suggesting that every Christian woman is directed to the vocations of matrimony and motherhood. In 1 Timothy 5 he says that older widows should embrace the apostolate of prayer and mercy instead of becoming entangled again in household cares. Since I believe with the Reformers that Scripture interprets Scripture, this passage is best understood in the light of 1 Corinthians 7:34 where Paul praises the unmarried woman or girl who dedicates herself exclusively to the service of the church. It should likewise be related to Matthew 19, where Jesus affirms the two distinct callings of holy marriage and holy celibacy and acknowledges that some "have renounced marriage because of the kingdom of heaven" (verse 12, NIV). The four unmarried daughters of the evangelist Philip, who were endowed with the gift of prophecy, appear to have embraced a vocation to celibacy (Acts 21:9), and Paul would surely have known of their ministry. We should also consider in this connection Revelation 14:4, where virginity is used as a metaphor for wholehearted consecration to Christ.[27]

It is indisputable that the epistles to Timothy place the spiritual relationship to Christ and to fellow-Christians over purely natural relationships. This is evident in 2 Timothy 2:4, where the apostle insists that service to the kingdom takes priority over all "civilian pursuits," a text that was later used to justify clerical celibacy. Moreover, in

1 Timothy we are told that within the community of faith, older women should be treated as "mothers" in Christ and younger women as "sisters" in Christ (5:2; cf. Matt. 12:46-50). Older women are not to be regarded as burdens on society, as we find in tribal patriarchy, but instead are to be given positions of special honor. The First Epistle to Timothy admittedly lends little if any support to radical feminists, but it also cannot justifiably be used to defend an autocratic or tribal patriarchy.

Some have argued that 1 Peter teaches the inferiority of women because they are described as "the weaker sex" (1 Pet. 3:7). Yet this is only a realistic recognition of the fact that women were in a weaker or more vulnerable position in the society of that time. It may also simply be an acknowledgment that the female sex is weaker in physical strength than the male. Instead of denigrating women, Peter exhorts husbands to "live considerately with your wives, bestowing honor on the woman." In fact he underlines the essential equality of husband and wife when he declares that they are "joint heirs of the grace of life."

Biblical faith condemns both male chauvinism, which exalts the man over the woman, and radical feminism, which denies the dependency of woman on man. It teaches the basic dependence of woman on man, as well as the interdependence of man and woman in relationships both in and outside marriage. It teaches subordination not so much of one sex to the other as of both sexes to the order or procession in which they find themselves. When it speaks of the subordination of wife to husband, this should be seen in terms not of servile submission but of creative service. It calls for strong, active Christians, and this includes all members of Christ's body (cf. Eph. 6:10-20; 1 Cor. 9:24-27). But when women are called to take initiative and assume leadership, they should do so as women, not as men or as sexless beings. The Bible has a high regard for femininity, even while it opposes the basic thrust of radical feminism.[28] It vigorously upholds a wholesome masculinity, even while it condemns male chauvinism. It affirms sexuality as a gift of creation (see the Song of Solomon), but it decries the perversions of sexuality as reflected in homosexual relations, adultery, incest, prostitution, and the tyrannical domination of one sex over the other. It has a high regard for marriage, especially marriage "in the Lord," but it sees faithfulness to God as having priority over the indissolubility of marriage (Luke 18:28-30; 1 Cor. 7:15).

3 / Women Ministers?

One of the raging conflicts in the evangelical as well as in the wider Christian world today revolves around the ordination of women to the ministry of the Word and sacraments. Those in the Wesleyan-Arminian tradition have been more open to women clergy than have those in the mainline Reformation and Catholic traditions. The Anglican church in particular has been rent asunder by this issue; it has proved so divisive that a new denomination has been born, the Anglican Catholic church. Eastern Orthodoxy has consistently prohibited women's ordination and maintains an inflexible stance on this issue today.

There is no gainsaying the fact that women were barred from the Aaronic priesthood of Israel. In Deuteronomy 16:16 we read that only males were designated to observe religious feasts. While not excluded from cultic observances altogether (Deut. 12:12; 31:12; cf. Num. 6:2), "women were inferior participants, obeying rules formulated by men."[1]

Nevertheless, women assumed positions of spiritual leadership even in Old Testament history, and occasionally their decisions on theological matters weighed more heavily than those of men. Miriam, the sister of Moses, was a prophetess in her own right; she even dared to reproach Moses for his exclusive claim to divine revelation (Num. 12). Although she was sternly reprimanded, her punishment did not lessen her status in later memory (Mic. 6:4). It was the prophetess Huldah who authenticated the contents of the scroll found during the reign of Josiah (2 Kings 22:14-20). Deborah was both a prophetess and a judge who ruled over the kingdom of Israel (Judg. 4:4, 5). It is well to note that the literal rendering of Psalm 68:11 is: "Great is the company of those women who publish the word of the Lord."[2]

We must also not discount the role of the queens of Israel, as well as the mothers of the kings, who often participated in governing the people. It should be borne in mind that the kings were not simply civil leaders but spiritual leaders. They were given the task of guiding their people in the spiritual sense and have therefore aptly been called "shepherd kings." Likewise, their wives and on some occasions their mothers functioned as shepherdesses. Certainly Bathsheba played a pivotal role in Solomon's accession to power as she worked in collaboration with the prophet Nathan (1 Kings 1:11ff.). Esther was a queen in a foreign kingdom, who nonetheless came to exert spiritual authority over her own people, the Jews. Queen Jezebel was both a theologian and a missionary, even though she chose to serve Baal over Yahweh. Like Elijah, she was perceptive enough to recognize the incompatibility between Baalism and Yahwism. Though she deserved the death she received, she met it with boldness and resoluteness.

As we turn to the New Testament, we read of the remarkable women associated with Jesus' birth. The prophetess Anna spoke of Christ "to all who were looking for the redemption of Jerusalem," and she gave her message in the temple (Luke 2:36-38). Both Mary and Elizabeth were chosen to bear sons of destiny; John the Baptist was to be the prophet who prepared the way, and Jesus Christ was the long-awaited Messiah of Israel. Because Mary was anointed to become the mother of grace, her position is preeminent over that of the apostles themselves, who were at the most heralds and ambassadors of grace.

Jesus was remarkably open to the possibility of women in ministry. He chose to reveal the mystery of the gospel, as well as his Messianic identity, to an unknown Samaritan woman (John 4). As "the enlightened one," she was sent out to become the first evangelist to the Samaritans.[3] In the conflict between Mary and Martha (Luke 10:38-42), Jesus decided in favor of the continuing right of women to full discipleship. Moreover, in his resurrected state he appeared first to Mary Magdalene and Mary, the mother of James, and commissioned them to go and tell the disciples about the good news of his resurrection (Matt. 28:1-10).

We are often reminded by those who hold to an exclusive male priesthood that Jesus named only men to be his disciples. While this is true, we should remember one possible reason for this: the disciples had to live and work together in close proximity, and the society of that time would not have tolerated the mixing of the sexes in this way. Many of the disciples were already married, and false scandals would have arisen that would have undercut Jesus' mission at the very beginning. At the same time, it should be recognized that on occasion groups of women accompanied Jesus and his disciples on their missionary journeys (Luke 8:1-3; Mark 15:40, 41), and that women were present in the upper room when Christ poured out his Holy Spirit upon the company of believers and so empowered them for ministry (Acts 1:14). Some medieval theologians referred to Mary Magdalene as the apostle to the apostles (*apostola apostolorum*), since according to the Fourth Gospel she saw the risen Christ first and then told the others.

Paul's attitude toward women in leadership positions is especially significant, for it was mainly through his missionary efforts that Christianity expanded into the Graeco-Roman world. It is incontestable that the churches under his jurisdiction accepted female as well as male leaders (see Rom. 16:1, 3, 6, 12, 15). On one occasion he even likens the apostles' supervision of churches in their charge to that of "a mother caring for her little children" (1 Thess. 2:7, NIV).[4] In Philippians 4:2, 3 he commends Euodia and Syntyche as "women [who] have labored side by side with me in the gospel." There is no suggestion that their labor differs from that of their male colleagues. Priscilla seems to have been at least the equal of her husband Aquila in their joint work as teachers (Acts 18:2, 18, 26; 1 Cor. 16:19; Rom. 16:3). In Romans 16:2 Paul requests that all Roman Christians, male and female, be at the disposal of the deaconess Phoebe "in whatever she may require from you." In this same chapter Paul alludes to "Andronicus and Junia, my kinsmen and my fellow prisoners who are of note among the apostles" (Rom. 16:7, KJV). The identity of Junia or Junias has been a subject of debate, but it is well to note that some of the early church fathers, including John Chrysostom, firmly maintained that Junia was a woman.[5]

The work of Phoebe is especially relevant to our discussion, since it appears that she did not function merely as a patroness or helper, but that she held an office in the church, involving the apostolate or ministry of evangelism.[6] While there is no scholarly consensus on this matter, her work certainly prepared the way for the ministry of deaconesses in the early Catholic and Orthodox churches. John Chrysostom notes in his *Commentary on the Epistle to the Romans* that Paul accepted Phoebe as an ordained deaconess. Origen goes so far as to acknowledge in his commentary on the passage on Phoebe that apostolic authority is given for the appointment of women ministers in the church.[7]

Against this open and advanced view on women's leadership, there are other passages in the Pauline corpus that seem to contradict this position. In 1 Timothy 2:12 Paul says: "I permit no woman to teach or to have authority over men; she is to keep silent." It appears that the duties of women are to be focused on child-rearing and household care (cf. 1 Tim. 2:15; Titus 2:5). As has been indicated, this passage should not be interpreted as a universal injunction against women in ministry; indeed, in the Second Epistle to Timothy Paul sends greetings to Priscilla and Aquila, who are both engaged in the teaching ministry (2 Tim. 4:19; cf. Acts 18:26). In that same epistle, Timothy's grandmother, Lois, and his mother, Eunice, who had instructed him in the way of salvation, are warmly commended (2 Tim. 1:5; 3:14, 15). In 1 Timothy 3:11 Paul acknowledges the ministry of deaconesses who, he says, must be "serious . . . temperate, faithful in all things."[8] It seems that Paul's injunction must be understood in its cultural and historical context: prophetesses connected with heretical movements were beginning to exert undue influence in the churches. The apostle may be reminding the women in the churches under his jurisdiction not to neglect child-rearing and household duties, so that "no one will malign the word of God" (Titus 2:5, NIV) or "give the enemy . . . opportunity for slander" (1 Tim. 5:14, NIV).

Paul's comments in 1 Corinthians 14:34 should be treated in a similar manner: "As in all the congregations of the saints, women should remain silent in the churches. They are not allowed to speak, but must be in submission, as the Law says" (NIV). This passage is especially perplexing, since in the very same epistle Paul acknowledges the right of women to pray and prophesy publicly in the assembly of the congregation (11:5, 13). Again, we must examine this passage (14:34) in its concrete context (*Sitz im Leben*). Paul is concerned about the growing anarchism in the services of public worship, in which speaking in tongues is being elevated above preaching and prophecy. Since it seems that it was mainly women who were involved in tongue-speaking, this was very likely a political stratagem to curb the practice of glossolalia in public worship. Moffatt comments that as Paul was about to close this portion of his letter, he might have received new reports of disorders in the worship services of the church fomented by woman members, and was therefore prompted to call for drastic action. Some commentators hold that verse 34 is an insertion of a later writer reflecting a hardening of attitudes towards prophetesses toward the end of the first century. My position is that these are the genuine words of Paul, but that they are not to be understood as unconditional or universal commands.

Another possible interpretation of 1 Corinthians 14:33-35 is suggested by Elizabeth Tetlow.[9] Paul is clearly forbidding women to "speak," but not necessarily to "teach" or "preach" in the liturgical assembly. It may well be that Paul's injunction refers to "unnecessary talking" rather than to any official function in the church. If this is a correct interpretation, it reinforces the view previously expressed that Paul's intention is not to issue universal directives, but to bring stability into the worship life of the congregations in Corinth.

Other books of the New Testament generally give positive recognition to women as witnesses and ambassadors of Jesus Christ. In Acts we read how Lydia, one of Paul's converts, opens her home so that people can come to be instructed in the faith (16:14, 15, 40). One interpreter comments that it is likely that her ministry went beyond being hospitable; she was probably one of those whom Paul mentioned as having "labored side by side with me" (Phil. 4:3).[10] In this same book Priscilla is reported as correcting the doctrine of Apollos (Acts 18:26), a man whom Paul called his equal (1 Cor. 3:5-9).[11] We are also informed in Acts that Philip, the missionary, had four unmarried daughters who were prophetesses and who undoubtedly shared in his ministry of evangelism (Acts 21:9). The Epistle to the Hebrews upholds Sarah and Rahab as women of considerable heroism and as models for the community of faith (11:11, 31). Some scholars, including Harnack, have suggested that Priscilla may well have been the author of this epistle. The First Epistle of Peter reminds the Christian wife that she is to be an evangelist in her own home and through her example may win her unbelieving husband to the Lord (3:1, 2). Women continued to assume church leadership toward the end of the first century, as is confirmed in the Book of Revelation where John inveighs against a Christian prophetess who is the leader of what he considers a false (and perhaps gnostic) Christian libertinism (2:20-23).

The most important theological reason for opening the door to the ministry of women is the doctrine of the priesthood of all believers, which was anticipated in the Old Testament (Exod. 19:6; Isa. 61:6) and fully affirmed in the New. In contradiction to the Aaronic priesthood which admitted only males, the royal priesthood (1 Pet. 2:9) includes all members of Christ's body. The Epistle to the Hebrews makes it clear that the sacrificial system of the Old Testament has been superseded and fulfilled in the once-for-all sacrifice of Jesus Christ. The believer can now enter the sanctuary of God's presence through the blood of Christ and no longer needs the special mediation of a priestly caste. Whereas in Judaism priesthood was hereditary through the tribe of Levi, in the New Testament church one becomes a priest by being united through faith with the one Mediator, Jesus Christ. Because we are brothers and sisters in Christ, we share in his priestly role by offering spiritual sacrifices to God (1 Pet. 2:5). By his Spirit all Christians are enabled to intercede, sacrifice, and counsel on behalf of others (cf. Rev. 1:6; Exod. 19:6; Isa. 42:6, 7; 61:6). All members of Christ's body have been anointed by the Spirit to be witnesses and ambassadors of Christ. Not only the sons of Israel but its daughters will prophesy; not only menservants but maidservants will give public testimony to the faith (Acts 2:17, 18).

The priesthood of all believers receded into the background in the patristic and medieval periods, but it was rediscovered by the early Luther and the Pietist Philip Spener, both of whom maintained that all Christians may speak in public assembly, all may hear confessions and give assurance of forgiveness, all may baptize and preside at the Lord's Supper in principle. The right of women to participate fully in the celebration of worship owes much to the sixteenth-century Reformation and even more to seventeenth- and eighteenth-century evangelical revivalism.

In the early church period the ministry of women, particularly in the form of prophetesses and deaconesses, was still highly visible. The second-century Acts of Paul portrays Thecla as a female missionary with shorn hair (24:40-43). Tertullian suggests that she had become a model for women who wanted to teach and baptize.[12] Women ministers were especially prominent among the Montanists who, despite their doctrinal deviations, made a genuine attempt to recover the spontaneity and charismatic enthusiasm of the early New Testament church in the face of growing sacerdotalism and ecclesiasticism.

The rise of an ascetic and mystical spirituality drawing upon Neoplatonism and to a lesser degree Manichaeism did much to undermine the role of women in the church, and this spirituality became a major force in the later patristic and medieval periods. It was said that only men were created directly in the image of God, and women indirectly, since woman proceeded from man. It was claimed that since Jesus chose only males to be his apostles, women are forever barred from the sacramental ministry. Pelagius wrote that it is contrary to the order of nature, or of law, that women should speak in the assembly of men.[13] For Thomas Aquinas, it seemed that the only thing woman is really good for is the work of generation, "since a man can be more efficiently helped by another man in other works."[14] The Spanish Dominican Dominic Soto (1494-1560), who reflected sixteenth-century Catholic opinion, held that the female sex presents a natural impediment to the reception of Holy Orders because of its poverty of reason and softness of mind.

In the developing Catholic piety, there was a flight from woman reflecting also a flight from sexuality (and ipso facto a flight from humanity). Celibacy and virginity were seen as more meritorious than marriage, and marriage was permissible only for the sake of begetting children, who hopefully would become celibates (Bernard of Clairvaux). The Pauline injunction that in the Lord "woman is not independent of man nor man of woman" (1 Cor. 11:11; cf. 7:14) was surprisingly disregarded by many leading spiritual writers as well as theologians.

Despite the rampant sexism that pervaded Catholic spirituality, many women nonetheless attained positions of spiritual leadership and honor. Women martyrs and confessors in the early church period came to be regarded as models of piety as well as heavenly intercessors and mediators whose prayers were solicited for healings and other miracles. Some women of renowned piety in their commitment to the reform of the church became critics of and counselors to popes, kings, and emperors. Bridget of Sweden, Catherine of Siena, and Teresa of Avila are striking examples; the latter two have in recent years been named doctors of the church. St. Margaret of Scotland in the eleventh century was both a holy woman and a queen; she functioned as a spiritual as well as a civil head of her nation. Besides her political and charitable activities, she presided over important ecclesiastical synods which separated the Celtic church from its old practices and brought it into line with the rest of Christendom. We should also recognize that not a few of the fathers and doctors of the Catholic church were sons of strong-minded Christian mothers. St. Monica, mother of Augustine, is an obvious example, since her witness and prayers had much to do with her son's conversion.

The unique role of the medieval abbesses should also be taken into account.[15] Between the seventh and ninth centuries, the abbesses ruled over the clerical and monastic houses as well as the convents of sisterhoods. Not only laymen but priests were under their jurisdiction. Some of these abbesses also had jurisdictional authority over civil affairs. Many of them presided at worship services and even heard confessions. Their right to rule was not questioned until the Renaissance, when an attempt was made to rehabilitate Graeco-Roman culture in which women had a lower status than in Christian times.[16]

While prohibiting the ordination of women to the sacramental ministry of the church, the Eastern Orthodox churches have nonetheless acknowledged the role of women as confessors and spiritual directors. A number of women have come to be recognized as "equal to the apostles" (*isapostolos*). Among these are St. Mary Magdalene; the martyr Thecla; St. Helena, mother of the Emperor Constantine; and St. Nina, the missionary who converted Georgia.

At the same time, Orthodox spirituality has been tainted by a Neoplatonic denigration of the material world. As in Roman Catholicism, women came to be seen as the inferior sex, and the great saints who happened to be women were considered exceptions to the rule. Clement of Alexandria reflected the emerging attitude in the patristic era when he declared that "every woman should blush at the thought that she is a woman."[17] Mount Athos, the famed monastic state in the Aegean Sea, has barred from its premises not only all female human beings, but also female animal pets. This prohibition extends even to men with long hair because of their resemblance to women.

Though the Reformation opened the door to the ministry of women by its affirmation of the priesthood of all believers, the ministry of the Word and sacraments continued to be closed to women. By its much needed but sometimes unduly harsh attacks upon Mariology, the doctrine of the saints, and the conventual life, the Reformation prepared the way for a more consistent and rigid patriarchalism in which the feminine element in religion was virtually suppressed.[18]

This is not to deny the solid gains that the Reformation effected in restoring the sanctity of home and family life. Marriage and motherhood were once again seen as worthy vocations, but they were understood within the framework of the old patriarchalism. To be sure, such men as Luther had a positive attitude toward the life of married love, viewing it as a glorification of God and its joys as a celebration of God's goodness; at the same time, marriage was basically understood not as a companionship in ministry (as among the later Puritans), but as a remedy for sin. The married and family life of both Luther and Calvin was, for the most part, exemplary; the practice of mutual submission can be seen in Luther's frequent reference to his wife, Katherine von Bora, as "My Lord Katie." Yet the Reformers failed to escape the repressive patriarchalism of their time, typified by this remark of Luther's: "What if women should die in childbirth? That is what they are here for, to have children."[19]

It remained for the later evangelicals (Pietists, Puritans, Quakers) to give women their due recognition as full members of the body of Christ. Among these post-Reformation movements of spiritual purification, marriage came to be seen as a covenantal relationship in which both partners regarded their primary vocation as the service of the kingdom of God.[20] In the churches of the evangelical revival, women began to attain noteworthy status as missionaries, and indeed account in no small measure for the rapid missionary expansion in Protestantism in the eighteenth and nineteenth centuries. What is not so well-known is that a great many of these missionary women were inwardly pledged to celibacy.

The advance of evangelical Protestantism is in part the story of the dedication of its illustrious women. In the eighteenth century Lady Huntingdon, an evangelical Methodist, sponsored about sixty chapels in the British Isles and financed a seminary for ministers known as the Trevecca house. Dora Rappard (d. 1923) served with her husband in directing the St. Chrischona Pilgrim Mission in Basel, Switzerland, an evangelical training school for home and foreign missions; she became known as "the mother of St. Chrischona" through her spiritual counsel, leadership gifts, and extensive writing.[21] Toward the end of the nineteenth century, Amy Carmichael, who had previously been a lay gospel preacher in the Presbyterian church in Northern Ireland, received the call to mission work in India, where she organized and led the famed Dohnavur Fellowship, a religious community dedicated to intercessory prayer and evangelism. Helen Barrett Montgomery (d. 1934), the only woman to translate the Greek New Testament into English, served as president of both the Women's American Baptist Foreign Mission Society and the Northern Baptist Convention.

The gift of prophecy reappeared among the women of the evangelical revival. In the Community of True Inspiration (the Amana Society), coming out of German Pietism, Barbara Heinemann attained special renown as a *Werkzeug* or prophetess. Seventh-Day Adventism was, for the most part, the product of the vision and labor of the prophetess Ellen White, who is generally acknowledged as the leading theological authority in that church after Holy Scripture.

The Holiness movement, which arose in the nineteenth

century, gave special recognition to the role of women in positions of spiritual leadership and authority.[22] Alma White founded the Pillar of Fire church, and Evangeline Booth became the celebrated general of the Salvation Army. Amanda Smith, born a black slave, received international acclaim as a missionary evangelist, preaching in England, India, Africa, and many other parts of the world. In Pentecostalism, whose spiritual and theological roots are in the Holiness movement, women from the very beginning have played a major role, serving as pastors, evangelists, healers, and prophetesses.

With the recovery of the monastic life in contemporary Protestantism, women have again attained positions of authority over religious houses. Klara Schlink, sister of Lutheran theologian Edmund Schlink, helped to found the Evangelical Sisterhood of Mary in Darmstadt, Germany, where she is presently one of the two mother superiors. This is not only a contemplative but also a mission-oriented foundation, and has become one of the centers of Christian renewal in our day.

While there have been sociological reasons, sometimes valid and sometimes invalid, for barring women from the ministry of the Word and sacraments, there are no compelling theological reasons. It is understandable in the light of the rigid patriarchalism that characterized both Hebraic and Graeco-Roman societies that women were not encouraged to seek the highest positions in the hierarchy of the church. To argue, however, that because Jesus Christ was male, therefore the priest as "another Christ" should likewise be male has doubtful theological validity. It came to be believed in Catholicism that ordination, like baptism, confers an indelible sacramental character, and that the priest therefore has a privileged spiritual status over the laity. But this contradicts the biblical and evangelical doctrine of the priesthood of all believers in which all Christians have direct access to Christ, all can hear confession and give absolution, all can preach and baptize in principle. Evangelicals insist, of course, that only those with the proper gifts should be certified by the church to serve in the ministry of the Word and sacraments. But this means that the clergy differ from the laity only in their function, not in spiritual status or moral worthiness. Thomas Aquinas contended that a bishop should be in a state of perfection, since his office requires a special measure of holiness. The question remains: Why cannot woman attain this special holiness as well as man?

It is sometimes said by Roman and Anglo-Catholics that we should trust the sacred tradition of the church which has in its supreme wisdom excluded women from the apostolic succession, though it has permitted women to serve in auxiliary ministries such as deaconesses. While it is true that no woman has ever received "the indelible character" conferred by ordination, at least in the Roman Catholic and Eastern Orthodox churches, this is an objection based on sociological, not theological, considerations. Why cannot women today receive the apostolic benediction by the laying on of hands, even if this has not been done in the past? As one who stands in the evangelical and Reformed tradition, I hold that the real apostolic succession is one of doctrine. All who adhere to the apostolic message stand in the apostolic succession, and all are commissioned to share the apostolic message with others, though not all are called to be public witnesses of the Word.

Man, to be sure, is the spiritual head in the household, but woman participates in this spiritual leadership by virtue of being one flesh with her husband (cf. Eph. 5:31; 6:2). Moreover, in the family of the church women may well assume positions of leadership over men by virtue of special tasks to which they are called and the spiritual gifts which they are given. The fifth commandment says that honor should be conferred upon our mothers as well as our fathers, and it is not unwarranted to use this text to argue that honor be given to mothers in the faith as well as fathers in the faith (cf. Heb. 11). As the wife of her husband, the woman is obligated to serve and support him as a helpmate in the Lord. But as a sister in Christ, she has equal spiritual status with her husband. If her mate is only a pre-Christian or a carnal Christian and she is a mother in the faith, then she is the source of spiritual authority in the household. If both parents are not yet in the faith or if they fall away from the faith, then their children, if they are committed Christians, become the spiritual directors in the family. Such children are still obligated to respect and honor their parents by virtue of the order of creation. Yet in the order of redemption, their voice has a certain priority, because their spiritual loyalty is not to their parents, but to their holy mother, the church, and to their heavenly Father.

While I acknowledge that women may take positions of spiritual as well as civil authority, it is necessary to insist that women still remain womanly and not try to usurp the male role. Karl Stern astutely observes that women in religious orders, "such as Saint Teresa of Avila or Mother Cabrini, have often displayed a physical tenacity, a fighting spirit, a sense of practical affairs worthy of a male 'executive type'—and yet that certain sense of the womanly is invariably there, in between the lines as it were."[23] Stern contrasts these saints of the church with Ibsen's Hedda Gabler, a representative of modern feminism, where one has a sense of the perversion or denial of womanhood. A woman pastor should not seek to suppress the feminine element within her in order to fulfill the responsibilities of leadership. The distinction between masculinity and femininity, which has its source in creation, is not overcome when women assume positions of leadership but, on the contrary, should be more visible.[24] The masculinization of women and the feminization of men is one of the tragedies of our age, and is in no small way responsible for accelerating divorce and the breakdown of the family. It cannot be denied that the women's liberation movement, for all its solid gains, has done much to blur the distinctions between the sexes and that many women who have entered the ministry appear to be committed to the eradication of these distinctions.

Because the movement for women's ordination today is so closely tied to secular ideology, and is therefore not always solidly anchored in biblical imperatives, my position on women's ordination is not an unqualified yes. One must be certain that women who are seeking to be ordained are motivated not by a commitment to the ideology of feminism, but by a commitment to Jesus Christ. What should be preached from the pulpit is not women's rights as such, but the gospel of reconciliation and redemption. Human rights should, of course, form a part of the church's proclamation (our mandate is to present the law as well as the gospel); yet this theme should never preempt the central message of the faith. A woman seeking ordination to the ministry of the Word and sacraments must also be committed to the sanctity of the family and the worthiness of the vocation of motherhood. The fact that some clergywomen today in the mainline Protestant denominations are championing the cause of lesbianism (and a few are even practicing a lesbian life-style) should give the church pause in its rush to promote women's liberation.

Paul's admonitions that women should keep silent in the churches are not completely passé. Karl Barth remarked on one occasion that a certain German woman theologian had best keep silent because her views were theologically and biblically subversive.[25] Modern prophetesses who denigrate the role of women as homemakers or who advocate abortion on demand, as do many modern feminists, should be told by church authorities to be silent in the public assembly of the church. Males, of course, who are in similar positions and who have fallen under the spell of a secular ideology should likewise be restrained by church authorities. The pulpit is not the place to promote an ideological cause, but instead is where God's Word should be proclaimed.

What is disturbing about the accelerating trend toward women ministers in the mainline Protestant churches is that they are regarded as being in a situation no different from that of their male counterparts. It is not recognized that there are peculiar problems, more of a sociological than a theological nature, associated with women clergy, and therefore special guidelines on this question are necessitated for presbyteries, synods, associations, etc. The fact that many women who seek ordination are married to a man in another occupation presents special difficulties that church authorities often choose to ignore. To encourage such women to be ordained may be to invite tension and discord in the family. A woman who has entered the state of holy matrimony has already made vows before God to serve her husband and to remain with him as long as both shall live. (Feminists occasionally change the wedding vows to read, "so long as we both shall love.") For a woman to be ordained under these circumstances means that the husband should give his consent only with the full knowledge of what this consent implies. Special counseling sessions designed to lead both parties to the right decision are certainly then in order.

Team ministries where both husband and wife participate in full-time church service would seem to be one way out of this dilemma.[26] The Salvation Army has pioneered in this approach, since its rules are that both husband and wife receive the same training for ministry, and both are given the same ministerial rank. If we would remain within the framework of biblical guidelines, the husband would have a certain precedence in authority, but the wife would certainly maintain the right to challenge him if she were the one who had the greater spiritual discernment. Where the husband is disabled either physically or spiritually, the wife in such a team would assume final responsibility.

My position is that in every family, and this includes the family of the church, there is finally one person who must be in ultimate charge. The Bible speaks of the pastors as shepherds who decide in consultation with others if the voice of God heard in Holy Scripture is contrary to the group consensus. The history of the church provides ample documentation that authority can be shared only to a certain extent, that finally one person must stand before God and be accountable for the people he or she represents. The modern idea of the democratic family where decisions are made on majority vote means that parents in fact abdicate their authority as parents. Likewise the pastor who receives his call directly from God and indirectly from the congregation is answerable first of all to God and then to the congregation. He is not a sounding board for the congregation, but a pastoral guide, a spiritual director. And in a team ministry one spiritual director will have the final say, though this does not mean that the husband and wife do not function in a genuine partnership.

This brings us to still another option for women who seek the ministry of the Word and sacraments—celibacy. Many of the early prophetesses and deaconesses in the patristic era of the church were pledged to celibacy, which gives the pastor a decided practical (though not a moral) advantage over his or her fellow-pastors who have obligations of raising a family. What makes this option unattractive to the modern woman is that the *Zeitgeist* of the culture ties personal fulfillment to sexual fulfillment, and the churches of Protestantism have always frowned on this alternative. It seems that women who in fact neglect their husbands and children, divorcees, flirtatious women, and even lesbians are often more acceptable to denominational executives than those who are pledged to lifelong virginity or celibacy. Such a state of affairs simply attests the nearly total secularization of the churches of our time. Women who seriously entertain the vocation of celibacy are certainly under an added obligation to dress modestly and to sublimate their sexuality without denying their femininity. Such women should also be open to the possibility of community life, since celibates are often troubled by the burden of loneliness. These women need not be lonely, however, even apart from a religious community; they can come to see themselves as sisters of men and women in the faith and as mothers of spiritual children. In the providence of God, they become special signs of the dawning of the new age where the primary ties that link men and women in the faith will no longer be natural but spiritual (cf. Matt. 12:46-50).

Women in ministry need a father confessor perhaps even more than men, since it is a formidable challenge to remain true to the faith in a society where sexism is rampant and where ideological feminism distorts what it means to be a woman.[27] The great women saints of the Catholic church almost invariably had spiritual directors or confessors of the opposite sex, and women pastors, especially those who embrace the vocation to celibacy, also stand in need of this kind of assistance. Those in team ministries have the assistance of their husbands, as men in the pastorate have the constant guidance of their wives, if their wives happen to be women of faith. Those in the auxiliary ministries of teaching deaconesses, sisters of mercy, and contemplative nuns likewise need the encouragement and support of their male colleagues.

Our brethren in the Anglo-Catholic, Roman Catholic, and Eastern Orthodox communions pointedly remind us that the present movement toward women's ordination in mainline Protestantism often lacks biblical legitimacy, that it more often than not draws its inspiration from ideological feminism. Mainline Protestants can counter Catholic objections to women's ordination by drawing their models for ministry from the great women saints of Catholicism (as well as of evangelical Pietism) who attained positions of spiritual leadership by denying themselves for the sake of the gospel. Like Jesus Christ himself and like Mary his mother, they were exalted by humbling themselves, they became leaders by choosing the role of servants. This kind of model contradicts the feminist ideal of the liberated woman, but it is the only biblically grounded model for the woman who seeks ordination to full-time service in the church. We can also urge our Catholic and Orthodox friends to consider that just as the Father delegates authority to the Son and Christ to the church, so it is not inconsistent with this biblical pattern for the congregation of faith to delegate authority to women seeking the ministry.

The present conflict concerning women's ordination to the ministry might be overcome if proponents would cease speaking of the *right* of women to preach and to preside at the sacraments. It is not any person's *right* to preach the gospel, not even those who have a Master of Divinity degree from an accredited seminary, whether they be men or women. Instead, the ministry of the Word is a *privilege* granted only by God himself, and the church simply recognizes and certifies this divine call. What must be insisted on is that God may call women as well as men to the apostolic ministry. To deny this is to place an unwarranted limitation upon the prerogatives of God, as well as to call into question those passages in Scripture that depict women in positions of spiritual leadership and authority.

4 / *Revising the Language About God*

Perhaps the major debate taking place in the mainline Protestant denominations today concerns supposedly sexist language in worship and theology. Feminists seek a more inclusive language for deity and call for a "resymbolization" of God. Patriarchalists and traditionalists resist this attempt to alter the core symbolism of the faith on the grounds that the meaning of the faith itself is then transformed. Feminist theologians propose a revisionist theology in which the guiding theological symbols of the past are reconceived in the light of the new consciousness of living in a male-female world.[1]

What is the more inclusive language favored by feminist theologians? Some suggest that we should drop personal categories altogether and think of God as the suprapersonal ground of being or the mystical abyss of silence. Those inclined toward deism have a preference for such metaphors as "Divine Providence," "Cosmic Benefactor," or "Source of Sustenance." Process theologians, who often share the feminist vision, maintain that God is best understood as "Creativity" or the "Creative Process." Some feminist theologians refer to God as a "fatherly-motherly force" or as a "creative force." Others recommend that we address God as "Father-Mother" or simply as "Mother." A few object that even "Mother" connotes a hierarchical world-view, that it is more proper to speak of

God as "Sister" in order to underline the fact that God too struggles for fulfillment in and with us. This reflects Whitehead's description of God as "the fellow-sufferer who understands." The feminist antipathy toward monarchism can be seen in one "progressive" hymnbook where "Lead On, O King Eternal" has been changed to "Lead On, O Cloud of Yahweh."[2]

A growing number of feminists propose that Jesus Christ no longer be thought of as Son of the Father, but instead as "the Child of God."[3] In addition, they object to calling Christ "Lord" and "Master," since these terms reflect a patriarchal vision. They offer instead the alternatives "Companion" and "Friend," which denote a relationship of mutual fellowship and equality rather than superordination and subordination.

In some feminist circles a distinction is made between *Jesus* and *Christ*. *Jesus* can be thought of as masculine, but *Christ* is depicted as feminine or neuter. Here we see a reappearance of the ancient Nestorian heresy in which the divine and human natures of our Lord are separated.

It is obvious from what has been said that feminist theology signifies a revolt not just against masculine imagery, but against hierarchical and dualistic categories as well.[4] In place of a monotheistic and Trinitarian deity, feminists are inclined to envisage deity in terms of a monistic world force or world soul. Some do not hesitate to affirm God as bisexual or androgynous (for example, Matthew Fox). Such usage reflects certain themes in early Gnosticism. Valentinus, for example, portrayed God as a dyad, consisting in one part of the Ineffable, the Depth, the Primal Father, and in the other of Grace, Silence, the Womb, and "Mother of All." Feminists, like monistic mystics, reject the concept of "Father in heaven" as anthropomorphic and mythological.

In radical feminism God is no longer the Father Almighty, but the depth or ground of being. He is no longer, as

Dorothee Sölle puts it, "the mighty One, the alien God who is wholly other, the One who commands"; instead God is likened to "the depths of the sea" in which one must be submerged in order to find life.[5] The prophetic vision is supplanted by a mystical one in which the discontinuity between God and his creation is blurred or denied. Carol Ochs expresses this very forcefully: "We, all together, are part of the whole, the All in All. God is not father, nor mother, nor even parents, because God is not other than, distinct from, or opposed to creation."[6]

Those who see themselves as the avant-garde of the feminist movement are increasingly calling for a new religion that draws upon contemporary experience as well as the experience of past ages. Naomi Goldenberg adroitly accuses the more moderate feminists of playing games, of not having the courage and foresight to break with the Judeo-Christian tradition, which in her view is incurably hierarchical and patriarchal.[7] She urges feminists to create new myths that are more in tune with the temper of the times and sees a fruitful source for this resymbolization in the current revival of witchcraft. For Goldenberg, God is basically a vital force within our physical and psychic life.

Feminists who are closer to the Christian understanding wish to alter the language and imagery, but not the meaning of biblical faith. Yet it can be questioned whether in their attempts at reconceptualization they preserve the basic intent of the biblical authors. Many, for example, prefer to speak of God as the infinite depth of being or ground of personhood as opposed to a divine person, but this tends to make God impersonal and suprapersonal. The same can be said for the appellation "heavenly Parent," which in effect substitutes a nonbiblical metaphor for an original biblical symbol, "heavenly Father." Such a term actually makes God less personal than "heavenly Father," since God is now made to seem detached and removed from the creature. The result is similar when "Creator" is substituted for "Father," as is the case in most so-called creative books of worship. This was the pathway followed by the deists and latitudinarians who sought to overcome anthropomorphic imagery, but the God that they ended up with was a God to whom it was impossible to pray, in the sense of petitions for divine aid. Prayer in the feminists' view is confined to praise and thanksgiving or simply reflection on the mystery of life. But prayer in the sense of bowing down before God and pleading for his mercy and favor signifies from their perspective a throwback to patriarchal and subordinationist modes of thinking.

Even evangelical feminists seem to be capitulating to the radical feminist ethos in their fascination with gender-inclusive language concerning God. Deborah Barackman, in a discouraging report of the Evangelical Women's Caucus meeting in Saratoga Springs, New York (June 1980), complains about

> the cavalier way the revealed names of God were treated in the desire to eliminate gender-specific language. There seemed little awareness that excision of titles such as "Father," "Son," and "King" does violence to his personal, Trinitarian, authoritative, and majestic nature. Though God "is spirit and not a man," to shift gender titles also confuses the relationships in such overarching scriptural metaphors as Israel as God's wife.[8]

The God of feminism is close to the God of Aristotle and Whitehead who moves the world by the lure of his (or "her") all-surpassing perfection. God becomes the magnetic attraction which spurs the "actual entities" toward fulfillment and completion (Whitehead, Hartshorne). This is a far cry from the God of the biblical prophets, who takes the initiative not only in creation but also in redemption, who intervenes in history and superimposes his will upon his people.

The God of the Bible is not part of the world process,

but the director of the process. He is not a passive Subject (as in both idealistic and naturalistic mysticism), but an Active Agent who reveals the majesty of his being in his condescension into human history.[9]

In some theological journals today, the policy is to cease referring to God by such personal pronouns as *he* or *him,* and instead simply to repeat the word *God* or use synonyms like *divinity. God himself* becomes *deity itself* or something comparable. In the case of adjectives, *his love* is replaced by *God's love* or *divine love.* Such a policy reflects not biblical theism, but a deistic or even Neoplatonic world-view in which God becomes detached or separated from humanity.

Mormonism seeks to overcome the difficulty by speaking of God as both "heavenly Father" and "heavenly Mother." But in the Mormon perspective, these terms refer to two different gods. Instead of Trinitarianism, we have a form of polytheism which is not very different from the mythologies of ancient Greece and Rome.

Feminism finds itself much more at home with mysticism and process thought than with any kind of polytheism or biblically-based theism.[10] Tillich's "God above God" or the "Eternal Rest" of the mystics are much more appealing to those who seek a concept of God that transcends or bypasses personal categories. Personality entails distinctions and relations, and such distinctions are an embarrassment to an ideology that is committed to overcoming dualistic and hierarchical models in favor of monistic and inclusive ones.

In attacking the feminist perversion of the faith, however, we must not be blind to developments in the theological and liturgical life of the church, both past and present, that have elicited the often valid protests of those who are concerned for the rights and dignity of women. It is true that the language about God in traditional theology has been so exclusively patriarchal that the feminist imagery concerning God that is actually present in the Bible is completely ignored. In our fear of pantheism and deism, we must not opt for a crude anthropomorphism (as in ancient Greek polytheism or in Mormonism) in which God is reduced to the superlative of human qualities. The Bible is clear that "God is not man, that he should lie, or a son of man, that he should repent" (Num. 23:19; cf. 1 Sam. 15:29; Hos. 11:9). The living God of the Bible, who is Creator of heaven and earth, cannot be subsumed under either masculine or feminine categories. At the same time, this God is the ground of both the masculine and the feminine, for otherwise God could not be described, even analogically. God infinitely transcends human limitations and human sexuality, and yet God created man in his own image as male and female (Gen. 1:27; 5:1, 2). God includes masculinity and femininity within himself, though not human sexuality; yet the God of the Bible is not androgynous, half male and half female. He includes masculinity and femininity as movements within himself, indicating initiative and power on the one hand (the masculine) and receptivity and loving obedience on the other (the feminine). In one respect he appears to be altogether masculine, and in another predominantly feminine.

The *masculine* and *feminine* are ontological categories which are not absolutely transcended in God, but which arise out of God. God as the initiator and determiner is the ground of the masculine, and God as the receiver and implementer is the ground of the feminine.[11] The difference between *masculine* and *feminine* is closely tied to the conception of God as a Trinitarian being. Otherwise God becomes a unitary being in which differences are excluded, or a cosmic force in which all differences are transcended. In the God of the Bible there is a diversity within unity. The debate over sexist language is ultimately a debate concerning the nature of God.

Feminist theologians are doing the church a signal favor

by causing us to reexamine the biblical imagery concerning God. Contrary to the assumptions of the old patriarchalism, it is evident that in the Bible God is not thought of exclusively in masculine terms. Patriarchal imagery is employed much more than feminine imagery, but both types of imagery are transcended, with neither being negated. The God of the Bible is neither "the Man Upstairs," nor "Mother Nature"; he is neither the Sky Father, nor the Earth Mother. And yet, analogies of gender are used to describe God in the Bible. Because masculine analogies coupled with metaphors of transcendence predominate, the biblical God is closer to the prophetic vision of the Sky Father than to the mystical depth of being personified in the Earth Mother.

Feminine imagery concerning God is especially evident in the Wisdom Literature, where Wisdom is depicted as a co-worker with God the Father in creating and shaping the world (cf. Prov. 8). Wisdom is still subordinate to God regarding function, though there are passages that seem to point to the essential equality of Wisdom and God. In this discussion we see the rudiments if not the foundation of the doctrine of the Trinity. In the Wisdom of Solomon, Wisdom is described as "a pure emanation of the glory of the Almighty" (7:25, NEB).[12] Again: "Like a fine mist she rises from the power of God, a pure effluence from the glory of the Almighty; so nothing defiled can enter into her by stealth. She is the brightness that streams from everlasting light, the flawless mirror of the active power of God and the image of his goodness" (7:25, 26, NEB). In Sirach we read: "I am the mother of beautiful love, of fear, of knowledge, and of holy hope; being eternal, I therefore am given to all my children, to those who are named by him " (24:18).[13] Wisdom is pictured in the Book of Proverbs as saying, "For whoever finds me finds life and receives favor from the Lord. But whoever fails to find me harms himself; all who hate me love death" (Prov. 8:35,

36, NIV). In this same book Wisdom is depicted as a "craftsman" by the side of God when "he marked out the foundations of the earth" (8:29, 30, NIV). Just as Christ is our Elder Brother, so Wisdom is described as our heavenly "sister" (Prov. 7:4).

In some other books of the Bible, feminine metaphors pertaining to God can also be detected. God is described in terms reminiscent of motherhood in Deuteronomy 32:11, 18 (cf. Ps. 131:2; Job 38:28, 29). On occasion, Isaiah employed female imagery to suggest the unfathomable love of God for a defeated people (Isa. 49:14, 15; cf. 42:14; 66:13). Christ likens himself to a mother in Matthew 23: "How often would I have gathered your children together as a hen gathers her brood under her wings, and you would not!" (verse 37). In the parable of the woman who found the lost coin, Jesus projects God in the image of a woman (Luke 15:8-10). In Matthew 11:19 we read in reference to the Son of Man, "Wisdom is justified by her deeds" (cf. 1 Cor. 1:24). Feminine metaphors regarding God are not usual in the Bible, but they are nonetheless present.

The biblical witness is clear that God is the ground of both masculinity and femininity. Even while transcending these distinctions, God also encompasses them. Yet we are not permitted to use masculine and feminine metaphors indiscriminately while speaking of God. It is not accidental but providential that in Scripture patriarchal and masculine imagery is used to describe the being and acts of God much more frequently than feminine imagery. In the Epistle of James, for example, even where God is portrayed as giving birth to his people he is nevertheless designated as "Father" rather than "Mother" (Jas. 1:17, 18).[14] Elaine Pagels underlines the monarchial and patriarchal character of the biblical God:

> Unlike many of his contemporaries among the deities of the ancient Near East, the God of Israel shares his power with no

> female divinity, nor is he the divine Husband or Lover of any. He scarcely can be characterized in any but masculine epithets: King, Lord, Master, Judge, and Father.[15]

Pagels contends that in the authentic strand of historical orthodoxy, God was conceived of in exclusively masculine terms, whereas in Christian Gnosticism God was thought of in both masculine and feminine terms. This is somewhat of an overstatement, since she does not take into account that such assuredly orthodox theologians as Hilary, Ambrose, Jerome, Augustine, Anselm, and Aquinas sometimes employed female imagery in the depiction of God.[16] Nor does she consider that the Bible itself does not describe God in exclusively masculine or patriarchal terms. Yet she is correct that the general thrust of biblical faith is to envision God as Sovereign Lord and Father Almighty, images that sharply differentiate the biblical vision from the Earth Mother of animistic naturalism, the Mother Goddesses of mythological religion, and the Eternal Silence of Neoplatonic mysticism.

The doctrine of the Trinity furnishes the key to ascertaining the dialectical relationship between masculine and feminine motifs in the action of God. This doctrine also enables us to discern how the God of the Bible transcends both patriarchal and matriarchal theologies. Karl Barth is right when he insists that in God there is "an above and a below, a *prius* and a *posterius,* a superior and a junior and subordinate."[17] The members of the Trinity, even though equal in essence, are divergent in function. The Son voluntarily subordinates himself to the Father, and the Spirit subordinates himself to the Father and the Son. This does not mean that the Father is exclusively masculine and the Son and Spirit are therefore feminine. Indeed, masculine images predominate for all three persons of the Trinity. But it does mean that there is a certain theological propriety in calling God the Father, just as we call Jesus Christ the Son. When Christ is associated with the eternal Wisdom that proceeds out of God, then it is appropriate to refer to Wisdom as feminine. The Spirit in his Pentecostal outpouring upon humankind is properly designated as masculine, but as the indwelling presence of God within the church, nurturing and bringing to birth souls for the kingdom, the Spirit may in this context be portrayed as feminine.[18]

Femininity is grounded in masculinity and not vice versa. This is the plain teaching of Scripture, and this principle applies to the Trinity, to the relationship between Christ and his church, and to man-woman relationships within the family of God and in the world. But as the masculine is the foundation of the feminine, so the feminine is the flower and fruit of the masculine, the glory of the masculine (1 Cor. 11:7). God is glorified in his people, the church, which is both the daughter of Zion and the bride of Christ.

It is well to give special consideration to the integral and inseparable relationship between Spirit and church. Significantly, the biblical imagery concerning the church, sometimes portrayed as the city of God, is overwhelmingly feminine. In Psalm 87 it is said of Zion, the city of God: "This one and that one were born in her, and the Most High himself will establish her" (verse 5, NIV). *The New English Bible* gives a poignant rendering of the hymn of praise directed to Zion: "Singers and dancers alike all chant your praises, proclaiming glorious things of you, O city of God" (Ps. 87:7, 3). The Second Epistle of John is addressed to "the Lady chosen by God" (verse 1, NEB). In some texts the church is described as our mother (cf. Ps. 87:5; Isa. 66:7, 8; Gal. 4:26; 2 John 1), and in others as the daughter of Zion (Isa. 1:8; 37:22; 62:11; Ps. 9:14; Lam. 1:6; Zech. 2:10; 9:9; Matt. 21:5; John 12:15). The woman in Revelation 12 represents both Mary and the church, the mother of the faithful. The Scriptures also commonly portray the church as the bride of Jehovah or as the bride of

Christ (Isa. 49:18; 54:5; 62:4, 5; Jer. 2:2; 3:20; 7:34; 33:11; Ezek. 16:8; Hos. 2:19, 20; Matt. 25:1-13; John 3:29; 2 Cor. 11:2; Eph. 5:23ff.; Rev. 21:9; 22:17).

The ground or source of the church is not in humanity, but in God. Indeed, the church is depicted as the New Jerusalem coming down from heaven, having the glory of God (Rev. 21:10, 11). Its living wellspring, its dynamic center is the Holy Spirit, who acts in and through the church to accomplish the redemptive purposes of God. When we call the church our holy mother, the reference is not just to the church as the field of the redemptive action of God, but to the church as the divinely-appointed channel of this action.[19] The motherhood of the church lies in its salvific role as the bearer of the light of the presence of God. By the power of the Spirit, the church receives and applies what is revealed by the Father through the Son. The supernatural fruitfulness of the church reflects the virginal fruitfulness of God in eternity, by which the Son is begotten of the Father and by which the Spirit proceeds from the Father and the Son.

As Christians, we do not bow down before the church as a human institution, for this is idolatry; but we should bow down before the head of the church, Jesus Christ, who includes the body of believers within himself, not just historically but ontologically (cf. John 15:1-8; Col. 1:18; 2:19; Eph. 1:13, 22, 23). We should also bow in reverence before the Divine Spirit who indwells the church and sustains it, who is its mystical center and ground.[20] Similarly, we do not adulate the Bible as a book, but we are called to revere the Word of God who meets us in the Bible, and who is in one sense inseparable from the Bible.

It is crucial to uphold the infinite qualitative difference between the divine and human, but at the same time I affirm that the finite is capable (through divine grace) of bearing the infinite (*finitum capax infiniti*). There is a divine side of the church as well as a human, and the same can be said for the Bible and the Eucharist. We should remember that the Apostles' Creed contains the words, "I believe in the holy catholic church." When the Reformers affirmed the infallibility of the church, they were referring to the church in its role as the mouthpiece of the voice of God, for infallibility as such can be posited only of divinity. This means that the church has a derivative or relative infallibility, one that exists only in the relationship between the church and its divine head or source, Jesus Christ.

To envisage God primarily as "Father-Mother" is in effect to deny the Trinity, since God is not a biunity or duality as this metaphor suggests, but a triune living God. Mary Baker Eddy, who used this phrase, thought of God in pantheistic, not theistic, terms. Julian of Norwich, the Catholic mystic who sometimes employed feminine imagery in reference to God, was always careful to refer to the first person of the Trinity as Father, even though she occasionally called Christ "our Mother." Zinzendorf, too, was accustomed at times to use feminine imagery to describe God, but he persisted in calling the first person of the Trinity Father and the second person Son, though he generally referred to the Holy Spirit as "our mother."[21]

It is my position that the context should guide us in determining the gender use in reference to God, and the context must be judged in the light of Holy Scripture. God in his relation to us as Creator, Redeemer, and Reconciler should always be referred to in masculine imagery, since these roles indicate power, initiative, and superordination. God is not male, to be sure, but masculine symbolism is nonetheless appropriate in reference to God in his mighty acts if we are to be faithful to Scripture and to the biblical and prophetic vision of the God who acts in history. Yet God in his relation to us as Nurturer, Guide, and Comforter may be envisaged as feminine. This is apparent in his role as the Spirit incarnate in the church.[22] It is also evident in his role as Wisdom, who is our providential guide, nurse, and counselor.[23] It might therefore be permissible on occasion to address the deity in terms such as "Holy Mother, Wisdom of God" or "Wisdom of God, our Mother," since such usage has some biblical support.[24] This terminology still reflects a dependence of the feminine on the masculine and the counter-dependence of the masculine on the feminine in order to realize the masculine goal. We must be guarded in our use of such language in public worship, however, since it is the church, not God, that is generally designated as feminine in the Scriptures.[25]

In Catholic theology the seat of Wisdom was transferred from the Son to Mary, and she increasingly became the feminine model for sanctity. It is said that the spouse of Christ is the church and that Mary expresses within Christ's spouse the divine motherhood.[26] This is not illegitimate, since Mary, too, as the mother of Christ and as the adopted mother of God, fulfills in a sense what is contained in the symbol of divine motherhood. Yet we insist that Christ also represents divine motherhood in his role as Wisdom who proceeds from the mouth of God accomplishing his purposes. As *Jesus Christ,* however, who assumes the roles of Savior and Lord in relationship to mankind, he is properly and necessarily designated by masculine symbols.[27]

The fact that Christ includes masculinity and femininity within himself does not warrant a change in gender language in reference to Christ. Because he has taken to himself the specific humanity of Jesus, the practice of referring to Christ as feminine and Jesus as masculine (encouraged by some feminists) is dangerously misleading and indeed opens the door to the heresy of Nestorianism.[28] This does not mean that Christ must be thought of exclusively as masculine, but it does mean that at least in formal worship and theology the common designation of Christ should be masculine.

To affirm, as do some feminists, that Jesus should be

referred to by the more inclusive symbol "Child of God" rather than "Son of God" is tantamount to denying his historicity. It is, indeed, to call into question his real incarnation, since he became incarnate in male, not female form. Just as some of those who were attracted to German Christianity at the time of Hitler tried to undermine the racial identity of Jesus Christ by representing him as cosmopolitan or even Aryan rather than Jewish, so feminists in effect disavow his sexual identity in their efforts to align the faith with a social ideology.[29] Unless Christ became incarnate in a specific human being, in a specific race, at a specific time, the underlying claims of the Christian faith are subverted. To deny specificity is to deny the incarnation, and to deny the incarnation is to deny the historical character of the Christian religion. We are then in the morass of a pantheistic mysticism which differentiates between the historical Jesus and the eternal Christ and regards the latter alone as the object of faith. Emil Brunner has aptly called the historical specificity of the Christian faith "the scandal of particularity," which sharply sets it apart from all monistic world-views.

At the same time, we must insist that though Jesus was indubitably a male, he was not a male without the female (the church). He represented the whole of the community of the elect, and not males only. So in a sense, when he was made flesh, it included the male and female form of flesh. The masculine in isolation is as much a denial of a Christian faith-orientation as the feminine in isolation or an artificial synthesis of male and female (androgyny).

Feminine imagery can be restored to worship and theology by rediscovering the church as our holy mother and Mary as the mother of all Christians. Protestants have lost sight of this dimension of the church by viewing it as only the gathered fellowship of believers, and not also as the very body of Christ. We need to recognize, as did the church fathers and even the Reformers, that the church has two sides—the divine and the human. It is divine because it is the body of Christ and the temple of the Holy Spirit. It is human because it is composed of sinful men and women. In its divine role it brings to birth children for the kingdom of God.[30] We therefore need again to think of the church as our mother.[31] In this way, we do justice to the motherly roles of both Christ and the Holy Spirit. We are also remaining faithful to the biblical language of Zion, which was inspired and adopted by the Spirit of God.

Church tradition has not been mistaken in viewing Mary as the personification of the spiritual motherhood of the church.[32] As the divinely ordained model of motherhood, she was elected by God to be the mother of his Son and of all those who belong to him. When Jesus gave Mary to his disciple John at the cross (John 19:26, 27), she became not only John's spiritual mother but the mother of all Christians.[33] As the mother of the church, she recalls to mind the role assigned to Wisdom in Ecclesiasticus as the mother of the faithful (24:18). Mary is not divine but is the sign and witness of the motherly dimension of the divine and as such is the model of motherhood for both Christian men and women. As Protestants we do not encourage the invocation of Mary, but in a certain context we may permit her veneration (cf. Luke 1:48) in the sense that all holy men and women of God can be held up as models of holiness and purity for the church at large. Because we as Protestants have been too quick to discard Mariology in our reaction against Mariolatry, we have lost contact with one of the enduring feminine models in the holy catholic church, a model that reflects not only human femininity but also the divine motherhood, which signifies at the same time the perfection of human motherhood.[34]

Closely related to this discussion is the extent to which the church is bound to the patriarchal language of Zion in describing God. It is my position that the revelation of God has been given to us in this language, and we can dismiss it for a new language dictated by current ideology only at the grave peril of losing the content of the faith itself. We cannot tamper with the core symbolism of the faith without ending in a new faith. The desire to revise the language of Scripture almost always leads to a revision of the biblical witness itself. Harry Blamires rightly observes, "There is no attack upon language which is not an attack on meaning."[35] Even Paul Tillich, who seeks to reinterpret the language of faith, acknowledges that we cannot escape from but must always return to the "original words" of the sacred tradition.[36] He admits that even words like "alienation" and "estrangement" do not succeed in capturing the full impact of the biblical word "sin."

I agree with Karl Barth and Hendrikus Berkhof that we cannot abandon the language of Zion or the language of Canaan. This is because the divine content is not given to us except in its human form. Moreover, I believe with the Reformers that the scriptural language is not just an accidental garb for the message of faith, but a divinely prepared and divinely inspired medium; and apart from this medium there is no message.

I also concur with Barth and Berkhof that the words "Father" and "Lord" in reference to God and Christ respectively are not merely figurative. They are not simply symbols of a power or essence which is beyond fatherhood and personality (as in Tillich and Mary Daly). They are analogies that contain a univocal meaning. The univocal in this case is not just the personal, as Paul Jewett implies;[37] it also embraces the element of omnipotent or absolute power which is a masculine, not a feminine, attribute. Some feminists argue that God is called Father, Lord, and Master in the Scriptures because analogies were simply drawn from human experience, and especially from human fatherhood, which always carries esteem in a patriarchal culture. Yet, as Barth rightly points out, God revealed himself as Father and Lord. He is not simply like a father; He *is* the Father.[38] Christ is not merely like a lord; He *is* the Lord. Barth sagaciously observes:

> No human father, but God alone, is properly, truly and primarily Father. No human father is the creator of his child, the controller of its destiny, or its saviour from sin, guilt and death. No human father is by his word the source of its temporal and eternal life. In this proper, true and primary sense God—and He alone—is Father.[39]

God as Father is an archetypal or foundational analogy, an analogy *sui generis,* since it throws light upon the human conception of father. The prophets and apostles did not impose upon God a conception drawn from their patriarchal society, but they received from God through his revelation the true and original meaning of fatherhood. God as Father is God's own witness to himself, not a mere human witness to God. This is also true for all the other foundational or key designations which God uses to describe himself and his love for his people, as Hendrikus Berkhof wisely points out:

> When the symbolical terms function in the context to which they belong, they are so relevant and transparent that we may no longer say that they are used in a "figurative" sense. For then they share in the true analogy as it is grounded in the creation and actualized in the revelational encounter. When certain concepts are ascribed to God, they are thus not used figuratively but in their first and most original sense. God is not "as it were" a Father; he is the Father from whom all fatherhood on earth is derived. The same applies to words like "Lord," "community," "love," etc.[40]

Thomas Aquinas, too, emphasized that the language of symbol applied to God's being and acts is not used figuratively, but is instead given its most essential meaning: "So far as the perfections signified are concerned, the words are used literally of God, and in fact more appropriately than they are used of creatures, for these perfections belong primarily to God."[41]

The criterion for deciding what analogical language is most appropriate is the self-revelation of God in Jesus Christ given in the Bible. To begin from human nature and experience and then posit in God the perfection of the creature is to end in the impasse of natural theology. This is the path taken by both ideological patriarchalists and feminists; it has also been the course followed by German Christians and Christian Marxists, who have sought to read into the faith their own ideological commitments. The way of faith, on the other hand, begins with the Word of God in Scripture and listens to God's own self-witness, which comes to us in the form of analogy to be sure, but in an analogy determined by divine revelation and not by human wisdom. With Barth I affirm the *analogia revelationis* and the *analogia fidei* (analogies given in revelation and addressed to faith), not the *analogia entis* (analogies based on a rational analysis of human existence).[42]

Feminists complain that this approach practically enthrones a patriarchal world-view. This is not the case, however; for although revelation comes to us in the form of patriarchal imagery, it transcends this imagery radically. The ideals and values of cultural patriarchy are irrevocably transformed. Even the conception of Christ as Lord and Master is not in accordance with the values of human monarchy and patriarchy, since Christ realized his Lordship and kingship in the role of a servant.[43] He did not command his disciples to wash his feet, but instead washed theirs—much to the chagrin of Peter (John 13:1-17). Christ was exalted in his humiliation. His power was displayed through the weakness of the cross. And so it must also be for his disciples.

At the same time, I believe that the language of patriarchy was adopted by the Spirit of God in his writing of Holy Scripture because there is an abiding truth in patriarchy that cannot be lightly dismissed. Patriarchy preserves the biblical principle of an above and a below, of a first and a second, of headship and servanthood. To deny or erase these distinctions between the members of the Trinity or between God and man or between man and woman is to end in a pantheistic monism in which creaturehood is swallowed up in deity. It is also to end in a social egalitarianism where children have equal voice with parents, where egocentric individual goals preempt loyalty to the family, and where sex is no longer confined within the estate of holy matrimony. Indeed, it is to open the door to all kinds of sexual promiscuity and perversion. I am thinking here not only of adultery and homosexuality, but also of incest, sadomasochism, and bestiality. It means the end of the family as the guardian of traditional values and the centralization of authority in an all-powerful state with its virtually compulsory day-care centers, mandatory "value-free" sex education programs (where naturalistic norms supplant traditional moral values), and government-financed abortion clinics.

Some have suggested that God can just as well be described as "Queen-Mother" as "Father-King." Yet this again is to treat analogical language as only figurative or metaphorical in meaning. "Queen-Mother" can only be used to describe a pagan goddess who is finite rather than infinite and material rather than spiritual. The images of "Queen-Mother" and "Mother-Goddess" connote dependence on some still higher power. The image of "God the Father Almighty" suggests independence from all creaturely power. Here again we see the marked difference between biblical theism, which stresses the essential independence of the Creator from the creature, and pantheism, which identifies God and his creation. We also discern the gulf between biblical theism and panentheism, which stresses the interdependence of God and creation.

One can legitimately argue that a God who creates by

the sheer act of his will is more appropriately termed "Father Almighty," "Lord," and "Majestic King" than "Mother." When God is thought of *primarily* as Mother, we are disposed psychologically to think of creation in terms not of divine fiat or *creatio ex nihilo* but of emanation, since the child is formed from material in the mother.[44] The irresistible tendency is then to look for God within the depths of the soul or of nature rather than in particular events in history where God in his sovereign freedom has chosen to reveal himself. It is well to recognize that every analogy includes a particular nuance of meaning that has far-reaching practical implications not only for worship, but also for Christian life. We cannot lightly discard time-honored analogies that have the support not only of Scripture, but of sacred tradition as well.

I agree with the Eastern Orthodox theologian Kallistos Ware:

> God in himself is neither masculine nor feminine, since he infinitely transcends any such categories. Yet it does not therefore follow that we are free to apply to him whatever symbols we please. On the contrary, if we were to substitute a Mother Goddess for God the Father, we would not simply be altering a piece of incidental imagery, but we would be replacing Christianity with a new kind of religion.[45]

One feminist, Starhawk, similarly concludes that a shift in symbolism from God the Father to a Mother-Goddess means a new religion:

> The symbolism of the Goddess is not a parallel structure to the symbolism of God the Father. The Goddess does not rule the world; She *is* the world. Manifest in each of us, She can be known internally by every individual, in all her magnificent diversity.[46]

God is neither suprapersonal nor impersonal, but *personal* in the most authentic sense. Analogies have to be used to describe God, since he transcends the reach of human perception and conception. But these are analogies chosen by God himself in order to reveal himself in terms that we can understand. Yet, "when Scripture calls God our Father, it adopts an analogy only to transcend it at once."[47] God as Father, just as Christ as Lord, contains an infinite breadth of meaning that simply cannot be captured in analogical language. Yet partly because of such language, meaning shines through the mystery of God's self-revelation in Jesus Christ. To discard these so-called root analogies in favor of metaphors such as "Father-Mother" or the "Womb of being" or "fatherly-motherly force" is to end in a new religion. Some feminists frankly call for a return to the primal myths of antiquity with its gods and goddesses who all had more or less equal standing.[48]

Paul Jewett argues that to change the references to God from masculine to feminine would convert God into a female, whereas the true God transcends the masculine-feminine polarity. Jewett believes that we should remain with the generic *he,* because *she* is a feminine personal pronoun that can only have a specific connotation. Yet he is unhappy with the traditional masculine designations of God and looks forward to a time in the church when there may come a change in our language about God.[49] In my view, the scriptural language will always be normative and relevant because it is God's self-designation through the words of human authors. At the same time, I believe that this naive language of faith should on occasion be supplemented by language that makes clear that the God of the Bible is much more inclusive and transcendent than the humanly masculine or the culturally patriarchal. But this more inclusive language ("infinite ground of being," "the all-determining reality," "the unconditional," etc.) is not closer but further from the meaning of who God is and what he has done for us; such language must consequently be controlled by and subordinated to the anthropomorphic, realistic designations of Scripture.

In summary, I contend for a confessional over a revisionist theology. To revise the language of Scripture in the light of the new consciousness of the world as male and female, as Virginia Mollenkott, Thomas Parker, and others suggest, is to alter irretrievably the content of Scripture. Instead of revising the language and ipso facto the witness of Scripture, we must confess this witness—and in the language that is given to us in the Bible. This does not mean that we cannot interpret and amplify, but we should do so only when our thinking is controlled by the Word of God in Scripture.

I have acknowledged that Protestantism has been dominated by a too rigid patriarchalism that has denied the feminine dimension in religion, even when it is clearly set forth in the Bible. I have argued that patriarchal imagery was chosen by the Spirit of God for a particular purpose. Patriarchalism retains certain nuances of meaning that are necessary for the interpretation and communication of the prophetic and biblical vision. The children of Israel had to contend for the transcendence and spirituality of God, personified by the Sky Father, against the fertility cults of the Earth Mother.[50] So in our day, too, we need to uphold "God transcendent" (Karl Heim) against those who are bent on returning to a pre-Christian era dominated by animism and polytheism, as well as against those who advocate the perennial philosophy of mysticism where all opposites and differences are transcended in an Eternal abyss of silence. I side with Barth and Berkhof against Tillich and Hartshorne in upholding a God who acts in history, as opposed to a ground of being that is the depth of history or a creative process within history. With Pascal, I contend that the God of Abraham, Isaac and Jacob is not the God of the philosophers.

The God of the Bible is closer to the patriarchal God of Islam than he is to the God beyond God of Tillich and the Eastern mystics. Yet this true, living God, who embraces a fellowship within himself, also infinitely transcends the God of patriarchal monotheism. While he reveals himself as Lord and Father, he is like a mother in some aspects of his activity and like a brother or sister in others.[51] He is monarchial, but not exclusively so; he is also friend and confidant (though he is Master before he is friend). He is not only the absolute ruler of the world, but also the suffering servant who has identified with the world's afflictions. He is not only the infinite ground and depth of being, but the all-powerful being who condescends to our level in self-giving love. This is why he must be spoken of as Father, Son, and Spirit and not simply as God or the Godhead or the Absolute. The battle to retain the personal categories of Scripture in reference to God is at the same time a battle to preserve the Trinitarian faith of the church through the ages.

5 / *A Biblical Alternative*

In contradistinction to both feminism and patriarchalism, I propose the biblical alternative of God's covenant of grace. One can refer to this position as covenantalism, so long as it is understood not as an ideology bent on restructuring society according to the dictates of particular vested interests, but as an outlook on life that serves the gospel proclamation.

This covenantal view is based on the biblical conception of the church as the covenant community, but the Christian family as a church in miniature is to be understood in a similar way. *Covenantal* in this context refers to a relationship between male and female. Its foundation is the promise of God to man, but this is a promise that must be acknowledged in faith and obedience. To understand male-female relationships in covenantal terms is to see the two sexes as created for fellowship with God and with one another. It means that man cannot exist alone, that he can live an authentic human existence only in obedience to the commandment of God and in gratefulness for the promise of God given to all his children. It also means that man can only live a truly human life in coexistence with woman, who was created to be his covenant partner. Together they are set in the world to live a life dedicated to the glory of God and the welfare of humanity. Their life of service is based on the covenant or agreement with God at the time of their baptism or decision of faith to live wholly for his glory and not for their own happiness. This covenantal pledge is reaffirmed at the time of marriage, since marriage itself is seen as a commitment to kingdom service in a relationship of physical intimacy. Christian marriage is a sign of God's covenant with Israel and of God's love for his church.

Karl Barth, perhaps more than any other theologian of recent times, has recognized that God's covenant with the people of faith has far-reaching implications for male-female relations, and particularly for marriage. As he phrased it: "Humanity as fellow-humanity, here actualised in the encounter between male and female, and supremely in marriage, is the real witness . . . to the Alpha and Omega of the will and counsel of God, of His covenant with man."[1]

The covenantalist, as opposed to both the feminist and the patriarchalist, sees our vocation as determined not by sex or blood or race, but by faith. The goal is not to ensure the continuity of the family (as in patriarchy), nor to realize human potential (as in feminism), but to become a sign and witness of the new age of the kingdom, to be a herald and ambassador of Jesus Christ. It is not to embark on a career of our own choosing, nor to submit to a station in life that one inherits because of one's sex or place in the family hierarchy. Instead, it is to assent to an order and vocation of God's choosing which supersedes our responsibility to our immediate family and any loyalty that we might have to our own sex or peer group. Obedience to the imperatives of the kingdom takes precedence over the vocation of biological fatherhood and motherhood (cf. Luke 11:27, 28), though the latter are not negated, but are now seen in the service of the former.

Whereas feminism stresses the independence of woman from man and patriarchalism the submission of woman, Christian covenantalism stresses the interdependence of man and woman, as well as their mutual subordination. At the same time, it makes a place for a differentiation of roles, recognizing both the dependency of woman on man and the necessity of woman for man in the orders of creation and redemption.

The biblical alternative is a transformed patriarchalism, which seeks to retain the principle of superordination and subordination, but sees them in much different terms than does historical patriarchalism. The subordination to which man and woman are both called is a subordination to God which involves placing the glory of God before human happiness and the interests of our neighbor before our own. Headship is realized through service, just as Christ was exalted in his humiliation.

On the other hand, the biblical alternative can also be considered a transformed feminism, since woman is now seen as the covenant partner of man. Yet the covenantal view seeks not the emancipation of woman (from home and family), but her elevation as a fellow-worker with her husband and her brothers and sisters in Christ in the service of the kingdom. Her vocation is essentially apostolic, and her work at home and outside the home is to serve the apostolic mandate. The ideal is not autonomy and independence, but service to Christ and to the family of faith, even before her own particular family. Her loyalty to her spiritual bridegroom, Jesus Christ, supersedes her loyalty to her earthly husband, since the latter loyalty is relative, not absolute.

The family of faith takes priority over both the nuclear and the extended family, but the last two are not annulled for that reason, but instead placed on a sure foundation. When father and mother, husband and wife, brothers and sisters are united in a common vision and in common tasks that take them out of themselves, they discover a newfound unity at a deeper level. A family under the Word of God will be a family pledged to the good of one another and of the wider community. Such a family will teach fidelity as well as chastity and will therefore become a model of Christian holiness in the wider community. In tribal patriarchalism, the woman is pledged to remain faithful to her husband, but the husband is generally permitted affairs outside the family.[2] In ideological feminism, both parties in the marital contract are permitted a high degree of sexual freedom. According to Susan Foh, "in feminist theory, monogamous sex is unnatural; it is one of the bonds from which women need to be freed."[3]

The biblical or covenantal alternative still makes a place for role differentiation, since it sees the divergency as well as the complementarity between male and female. It affirms the fundamental equality of man and woman under God, but it nonetheless acknowledges a difference in roles rooted in both biology and psychology.[4] The woman alone can be the child-bearer, and she is especially equipped to nurse the child, though the husband can certainly share in the raising of the children. Yet in the covenantal view, the woman sees her vocation not simply as the bearing of children, but as the educating of children in the fear and knowledge of God. She is to be a mother in the faith even before she is a mother according to the flesh.

Similarly the husband, by virtue of the physical strength that enabled him to be a warrior and hunter as well as a tiller of the soil, became the breadwinner in the family. Because of the tremendous change in cultural patterns, both husband and wife are now equipped to work outside the home. Nevertheless, thanks to his relative freedom from child-rearing and related household duties, the husband still retains a certain responsibility in providing for and directing the family. This is a sociological observation, but theologically the husband is given the role of spiritual director and guide for his family (cf. Eph. 5:22-33; 6:1-4).

Yet even here a patriarchal model is severely qualified.

The headship of the husband in the family is not lording it over others, as in the pagan concept of authority (cf. Matt. 20:25, 26), but serving the members of his household not just as an earthly provider, but as a father or brother in the faith who genuinely seeks the betterment and happiness of all those in his care.

Because the Christian family is a church in miniature, it will be patterned after the community of faith which is under the direction of shepherds who are spiritually responsible first of all to God and then to the flock that is their charge. In the Bible the church or covenant community is also likened to an army, and not all can be commanding officers in an army. It is an army whose weapons are not temporal, however, and whose strategy is not the death of the sinner, but his conversion. It is an army that overcomes by "revolutionary subordination."[5] It persists in making its witness even at the risk of martyrdom and therefore defeat in the eyes of the world.

Just as the kingdom of God is opposed to egalitarian democracy, so the Christian family is opposed to the democratic family where all share equally in leadership responsibilities. The headship of the husband is not one of domination, but it is still headship in the sense of providing directions, offering guidelines. In the Christian family, the husband will not exclude the wife or even the children from policy-making decisions, and he will try to exert his authority indirectly by genuinely trying to serve the interests of the others. His headship will be a "veiled, loving headship" (Sheldon Vanauken).

Subordination in the Christian sense is not demeaning, but elevating. It signifies not servile dependence, but creative service. The subordination of woman to man is a parable of the submission of the church to its Lord. Those who reject this want the church to be equal to the living Lord. Rosemary Ruether repudiates the Christ-church analogy of covenantal marriage because it is a "hierarchical, dominance-submission model of marriage."[6] But she fails to see that in the covenantal relationship, the husband too is called to subordination—to Christ first of all, and then to his wife in his role as Christ's representative. In the covenantal relationship the husband does not assert his rights over those of his wife, but instead is concerned for the rights of all in his care. But neither does he deny or forsake his special role to be the guardian of and provider for the family, the shepherd of the flock that is his charge.

A very real danger in the patriarchal family is tyranny in which the husband uses his power to hold his wife and children in servile dependence and submission. The danger in the egalitarian or feminist family is anarchy or even matriarchy in which the resulting vacuum in leadership is then filled by the wife or the children. Patriarchy calls for male supremacy. Feminism calls for female autonomy. Covenantalism calls for male-female partnership under the Lordship of Jesus Christ.

This means that major decisions in the family are to be made wherever possible by mutual agreement between husband and wife as they prayerfully seek the guidance of the Holy Spirit. The wife will defer to her husband, however, if he definitely feels that he is being directed by God toward a particular action. Yet she must not accept even this decision uncritically, for her first authority is the command of Christ given in Holy Scripture; she is therefore obliged to weigh even the resolution of her husband in the light of God's holy Word.

The precise relationship between male and female roles in a Christian family is illuminated by recalling the order of procession in the Trinity. Just as we see the principle of superordination and subordination in the Trinity (the Son is "begotten" of the Father), so we observe this principle at work in the world—in government and in the family. Just as we perceive a distribution in the actions of the Trinity in relationship to the world, so we see a complementarity in the roles within government and within the family. Yet because the members of the Trinity are one in essence, and because each person participates in the activity of the others, these roles are not to be conceived of legalistically or rigidly. The wife participates in the headship of the husband as spiritual director or father of the family, and the husband shares in the wife's headship as mistress of the house. These are not their primary roles, but neither partner is excluded from these roles. In exceptional cases, of course, where either husband or wife abdicates or is unable to fulfill his or her responsibilities, then the woman becomes "the man of the house," and the man becomes the helper of the woman.

The movement today toward complete egalitarianism, where equality is defined in terms of sameness rather than equal opportunity, signifies a revolt against the authority of Christ over his church. Christ and the church are not equals, and this is true for husband and wife, parents and children, in the sense that their positions in the family structure do not carry the same measure of authority and accountability. They are equal heirs to salvation, they are equally precious in the sight of God, but this is not to imply that all members of a family have equivalent gifts and responsibilities. In Arthur Cochrane's opinion, that side of the women's liberation movement which has developed into the ideology of feminism signifies a modern rebellion against all authority. The images of *father* and *husband* (as well as *mother*) are authority images. To call God *Brother* or *Sister* instead of *Father* (a practice which receives some support from the Presbyterian Advisory Council on Worship)[7] signifies a flagrant disregard of biblical authority.

The church has rightly become sensitive to the demands of women for equal pay and equal opportunity for work, but sections of the church have unwittingly allied the faith with a social ideology (feminism), which is basically hostile to the biblical heritage.[8] Naomi Goldenberg echoes the views of many modern feminists: "The feminist movement in Western cultures is engaged in the slow execution of Christ and Yahweh. . . . All feminists are making the world less and less like the one described in the Bible."[9] In her theology, nature is sacred, and reality lies beyond good and evil. She calls for the return of female goddesses to take the place of Yahweh, the monarchial god of the Hebrews.

An ideology might be defined as a vision of society which justifies or rationalizes the concerns of a particular interest group or class. It entails in addition to a theoretical system a definite sociopolitical program. Ideas are no longer abstract models of truth, but increasingly become instruments or tools in a program of social restructuring. An ideology in this sense is to a high degree socially conditioned, since it reflects the interplay of economic and other cultural forces. Reinhold Niebuhr, drawing upon the insights of Marxism, is right in speaking of an "ideological taint" to all human reasoning, because we cannot escape the cultural and economic pressures which impinge upon us. At the same time, as Christians we must always endeavor to transcend ideology and to bring every ideology under the scrutiny of the transcendent Word of God. Feminism is only one among several ideologies today, and a good case can be made that it reflects the mood of upper middle class men and women, particularly those in the professional and managerial class, who are bent on affirming personal autonomy and independence from traditional hierarchical values.[10] Other examples of current ideologies are classical liberalism (conservatism), welfare liberalism, socialism, communism, fascism, libertarianism, and patriarchalism. Feminism has a special affinity to welfare liberalism and socialism, whereas patriarchalism is often allied with conservatism and fascism.

In contrast to the biblical vision, feminist ideology regards subordination and obedience as anathema. Its revolt is directed against dualism and hierarchicalism, ideas that belong to the very center of the biblical interpretation of life and history. To begin with the "new awareness of a male-female world," as does Thomas D. Parker, is to impose upon the Bible an ideology. We all bring to the Bible an ideological bias, but to make this a hermeneutical principle is nonsense. In the biblical perspective the aim in life is not self-fulfillment in a career of our choosing (as in feminism), but the fulfillment of our vocation under the cross.

One of the hallmarks of feminist ideology is the commitment to gender-inclusive language in reference to both God and humanity. It is said that we should speak not of *men* or of *women,* but of *people* or *humans.* Instead of *mankind,* we should use the terms *humankind* or *humanity.* Instead of referring to God as Lord or Father, we should refer to God as the ground of being or the world-soul or the undifferentiated unity (as in mysticism). Inclusive language may well be in order in some cases. For example, it can be shown that the term *men* is now predominantly a specific rather than a generic term.[11] At the same time, the danger in gender-inclusive language is that it tends to obliterate the very real differences between men and women. Inclusive language does not necessarily overcome sexism. Why not speak of a woman who presides at a meeting as a chairwoman or as madam-chairman rather than chairperson? The former words enhance her womanhood, whereas the latter term implies an androgynous understanding of human existence. Instead of saying firefighters (in place of firemen), why not speak of firemen and firewomen, as does the women's liberation movement in Holland? It is not enough for women or men to discover their personhood; they must also discover their womanhood and manhood.

While there may indeed be some merit in the trend toward inclusive language, particularly where masculine terms generally no longer maintain a generic meaning, we must also consider with Harry Blamires the wisdom of the ages that somehow the masculine can contain the feminine, but not vice versa. Blamires perceptively points to "the myth of Eve's creation from Adam's rib" as an expression of this universal human awareness of the possible inclusion of the feminine in the masculine, which has shaped linguistic usage throughout history.[12] Yet if we would do justice to the biblical narrative, we must acknowledge that while man has a certain priority over woman, he remains woefully deficient apart from woman.

The Bible is unashamedly monarchial, but not sexist. It stands against the exploitation of woman by man, but it nonetheless speaks of superordination and subordination, of headship and servanthood, of an above and a below. It describes Christian marriage as a sign of God's covenant with Israel, in which Christ is the bridegroom and Israel the bride. In this parable the bride is dependent on the bridegroom, but the bridegroom in turn is glorified in and through the bride. The bridegroom does not try to keep the bride down but sacrifices himself for the bride.

An ideology, in contrast to a living faith, is intolerant and fanatical; it brooks no opposition. Its rigidity masks a basic insecurity and desperation, for its votaries are painfully aware that their attempt to create meaning for themselves is their only bulwark against emptiness and chaos. Unlike an ideology, faith can afford to dialogue in a spirit of openness, since it is confident that truth is invincible and that it will finally prevail. Whereas an ideology pins its hopes on human strategy and technique, faith humbly recognizes that truth does not depend on human efforts and arguments. While an ideology claims a premature possession of the truth, faith is content to wait for the full disclosure of truth in the future beyond history.

That most feminism is ideological in the foregoing sense

no competent observer would deny. Like ideologists on the left and right, the hardcore feminists seek to make people conform to their own perceptions of reality for fear that these could be shown to be erroneous if exposed to the light of truth. They cannot tolerate dissent lest their own vision of life be shown to rest on a delusion. The totalitarian character of feminism as an ideology is exemplified by Simone de Beauvoir:

> No woman should be authorized to stay at home to raise her children. . . . Women should not have that choice, precisely because if there is such a choice, too many women will make that one. It is a way of forcing women in a certain direction. . . . In my opinion, as long as the family and the myth of maternity and the maternal instinct are not destroyed, women will still be oppressed.[13]

Needless to say, patriarchalism, too, is an ideology which the church must be on guard against. Indeed, in one sense patriarchalism is more dangerous than feminism, because patriarchal imagery was used for divinity in the Bible and therefore appears easily reconcilable with the witness of faith. There is no doubt that the revelation of God was given in a patriarchal culture, but what is not always clearly understood is that this revelation transformed and overcame the oppressive and purely cultural elements in patriarchy.

The Hellenistic world, both Gentile and Jewish, was incurably patriarchal at the time of the advent of Christ. In contrast to the religion of early Israel, later Judaism increasingly hardened in its attitude toward woman, as can be seen in one of its daily prayers: "I thank thee, O Lord, that thou hast not created me a woman." In Graeco-Roman society the rights of the father, or paterfamilias, over his children were almost unlimited. The children literally belonged to the father, who could decide to abandon them in infancy to die of exposure or could later dispose of their lives at any time. The wife was reduced to the status of an unpaid housekeeper and nursemaid for the children.

Patriarchal ideas drawn from both the Semitic and Hellenistic worlds entered into theological speculation in the early church and medieval periods. Jerome maintained that the man should be commanded to love his wife, whereas the woman should fear her husband. Augustine wrote that only man is the image and glory of God, and that a believing woman is restored to the image of God only when she becomes a pure spirit. Ambrosiaster regarded woman as inferior to man because she is only a portion of him. Thomas Aquinas held that "woman is naturally subject to man, because in man the discretion of reason predominates."[14]

Against patriarchalism, evangelical Christianity says that one is not born into the kingdom, but one becomes a member of the kingdom by faith. It is not by procreation but by regeneration that one is inaugurated into the family of the church.[15] Our vocation, moreover, is not to ensure posterity for the family name, but to beget spiritual sons and daughters. Biological parentage is only a preparation for spiritual parentage.

What I am presenting as the biblical alternative can be seen as a qualified patriarchalism, but it is one that is radically qualified. In tribal patriarchy, the husband is a despot and the wife a virtual slave. The man-slave relationship is transformed in the Bible; this is especially evident in Philemon. Yet there still remains the difference between employer and employee. There is still a certain hierarchy in human relationships, not because of the patriarchal world-view of that time, but because God reveals himself as encompassing and at the same time transcending hierarchy.

In historic patriarchy the husband is the breadwinner and the wife the homemaker. Biblical faith affirmed this as a guideline, but not as a rigid law. Even in Genesis the so-called patriarchs shared in the wifely responsibility of caring for family and guests. Abraham helped in the preparation of the meal for the two strangers (Gen. 18). Lot baked the meal for the angels in Sodom (Gen. 19). Deborah and Esther, as well as the queens of Israel and Judah, assumed authority over men, and some of these women have been hailed as saints and heroines of the faith.

In opposition to patriarchy, biblical religion recognizes the right of a wife to reprove her husband, even in her role as a wife. This is still more true in her role as a sister in Christ, for she is essentially equal in spiritual authority. As a mother in the faith she may even have priority over her husband in spiritual matters, though she will not exercise this authority in such a way as to downplay or subvert her husband's leadership. A perceptive husband who discerns in his wife the manifestations of the Spirit will defer to her judgment on theological or spiritual questions. In sharp contrast to patriarchal ideology, Scripture asserts that a believing woman is not bound to stay in a marriage if her unbelieving partner threatens to leave (1 Cor. 7:15).

Christian faith does not negate the abiding values of patriarchalism, but points beyond them. The Christian wife will not just care for her husband and children (as in patriarchalism), but she will give hospitality to strangers, she will extend a welcoming hand to the homeless. Together with other members of her family, she will minister to the bereaved. Similarly, her husband will not just provide for his wife and family, but he will give to the poor, aid destitute widows, visit the sick, and perform other acts of sacrificial service.

In the biblical, covenantal view, authentic womanhood goes beyond being a wife and mother, just as authentic manhood goes beyond being a husband and father.[16] Obedience to the divine commandment sometimes means foregoing marriage and parenthood for undivided service to the work of the church (cf. 1 Cor. 7:25ff.). It may also sometimes entail marriage without children in order to accomplish a particular task given by God.

As has already been indicated, the biblical position can also be regarded as a qualified feminism. Yet in opposition to ideological or secular feminism, it takes for its criterion the divine commandment given in Holy Scripture, not the new light that is brought to bear on the current situation by the social sciences. It upholds as the ideal of womanhood not Eve, who symbolizes independence and autonomy, but Mary who epitomizes fidelity, humility, and absolute dependence on God. Its model is not the "liberated" woman, but the woman of modesty and piety, qualities associated in Hebraic literature with natural beauty. It preaches freedom—not from moral taboos that keep the social fabric intact, but from the expectations of one's peers or family or class regarding one's life-style and task in society.

The qualified, biblical feminism that I support stands in tension with the point of view of many of those who call themselves Christian feminists. While there are areas of convergence, there are also areas of divergence. Many Christian feminists will speak of submission and obedience to God or Christ, although their preference is to place the accent on cooperation with God and Christ. Their affinities are more to the God of process thought, the "fellow sufferer who understands," than to the monarchial, sovereign Lord of biblical faith. They also resist the idea of obedience to human authorities such as heads of state and church. Yet the Bible is clear that we are to give the human authorities set over us by God a relative, though not an absolute, allegiance. Christian feminists will speak of mutual submission, but not of the relative subordination of woman to man in the covenantal relationship of holy matrimony, nor of the subordination of both man and woman to the divine order which determines their place in the marital and familial relationship.

Biblical faith, particularly as we find it in the Pauline epistles, contends for a certain kind of subordination of the woman to the man in the covenantal relationship of marriage. This is not because she is inferior, but because she is endowed with those unique qualities that enable her to make the male complete.[17] Because her subordination entails among other things the task of propping up her husband, she may even be considered to have a certain superiority in this respect. By being the complement of the man, and particularly of the man in Christ, she realizes her own vocation of being a servant and witness to the God who created male and female in his image. Subordination in the context of Christian marriage does not mean a servile subjection to the male partner (as in autocratic patriarchy), but a willingness to accept his direction in the Lord and also a willingness to correct him, if this is the Lord's will. Mutual respect and creative interchange rather than domination and subservience characterize the kind of marriage that has the blessing of God.[18]

The polarity of the sexes is acknowledged in nearly all the great civilizations and world religions. In Taoism, they are understood as Yin (the feminine, which is calm, dark and receptive) and Yang (the male, which is active, light and generative). In the nations of the West, it is commonly thought that women are more intuitive and concrete in their perceptions, whereas men are more abstract and idea-oriented.[19] It is often asserted that women are inclined to be more perfectionistic and fastidious than men. Kathy Kristy sees the difference between the sexes in terms of "power and passivity, ebb and flow, generativity and receptivity."[20] We must be careful not to read into our conceptions of masculinity and femininity purely cultural elements that are always fluid and changing. At the same time, we should note that cultural ideas on this subject are rooted in the indisputable biological difference between male and female.[21]

Karl Barth is helpful here in warning against reducing male-female differences to a cultural standard, but he insists that the essential polarity of the sexes still be maintained:

> Of course, it is not a question of keeping any special masculine or feminine standard. We have just seen that the systematisations to which we might be tempted in this connexion do not yield any practicable imperatives. Different ages, peoples and cultures have had very different ideas of what is concretely appropriate, salutary and necessary in man and woman as such. But this does not mean that the distinction between masculine and non-masculine or feminine and unfeminine being, attitude and action is illusory. Just because the command of God is not bound to any standard, it makes this distinction all the more sharply and clearly. This distinction insists upon being observed.[22]

It is appropriate at this point to spell out a typology of male-female relations. Kate Millett in her *Sexual Politics* speaks only of patriarchalism and feminism, but there are other positions that need to be taken seriously.[23] Besides the biblical alternative, which I have labeled covenantalism, there are romanticism and naturalistic hedonism. Romanticism enthrones the love known as Eros, in which man and woman find in each other the ideal mate.[24] In this perspective it is not marriage and family, but love itself that is the object and goal of the human quest. To be possessed by or to possess one's beloved takes priority over obligations to family, church, and society. In naturalistic hedonism, it is sex that is idolized; intimate, caring love between the sexes is often seen as a hindrance to free sexual expression.

Kate Millett mistakenly subsumes naturalistic hedonism under the category of patriarchalism. Hedonism can take patriarchal forms, but the new naturalism is not to be confused with classical patriarchalism where man and woman are bound together in lifelong marriage under God. Patriarchalism is pro-family; hedonistic naturalism is anti-family. Patriarchalism stresses the reproductive purpose of sex; naturalism upholds recreational sex. Naturalism is a form of primitivism where woman is portrayed as the enticer and man the attacker; in this respect, it reflects certain motifs in tribal patriarchalism. Yet in its emphasis on the free expression of sex on the part of both men and women, it is more akin to radical feminism than to classical patriarchalism.

The gulf between the various positions is dramatically revealed by comparing the fundamental ways in which they visualize woman. The model of woman in tribal patriarchalism is the brood mare; in hedonistic naturalism, she is the "bunny" or plaything; in feminist ideology, she is the self-sufficient career woman; in romanticism, she is the fairy princess or maiden in distress waiting to be rescued; in biblical faith, she is the partner in ministry. In the biblical view, she may also be a mother—and yet never just a mother, but a Christian mother.

The conflict over this question may be expressed in another way. In patriarchalism, woman is the property of man. In romanticism, woman is the object of man's dreams. In hedonistic naturalism, woman is a sex partner for man. In feminism, woman is the rival of man.[25] In biblical faith, woman is the helpmate of man. Although in this last perspective man has a certain priority over woman, he does not have supremacy (as in the patriarchal view).

How women gain their liberation or salvation is also a subject of wide dispute. In patriarchalism, women are saved by childbearing. In naturalistic hedonism, women are fulfilled in the experience of orgasm. In romanticism, women are saved by being possessed by their knight in shining armor, the man of their dreams. In feminist ideology, women are saved by asserting their independence from the male-dominated social order or from family and clan. In biblical faith, women are saved *by* divine grace and *for* a life of service to Christ and fellow-humanity.

The tensions between the various positions are especially evident in the way they view marriage. In patriarchalism, marriage belongs to the order of necessity. It is basically seen to be in the service of biological fertility.[26] In naturalism, marriage is a convenience that may or may not serve the quest for sexual fulfillment and gratification. In romanticism, marriage is regarded as a possible threat to the mutual commitment of the two lovers because of children and other family obligations. In feminism, marriage is considered a contract that is intended to serve the ambitions of each partner. In biblical faith, marriage is thought of as a partnership in kingdom-service where children are wanted as co-workers in the kingdom and not simply as a means to ensure the family name or even to cement the solidarity of the family.[27] Here the purpose of marriage is not the perpetuation of families or the preservation of properties (as in patriarchalism), but the upbuilding of the covenant community.[28]

In contrast to patriarchy, Christianity regards marriage as being in the order of grace, not of necessity. Marriage is not intended for everyone or practically everyone, but only for those who have been called by God to this particular vocation. Like celibacy, marriage is seen as depending on the gift of a special grace (cf. Matt. 19:8-12). Marriage is enhanced when celibacy is presented as a serious option, because then marriage becomes a free decision, just as celibacy, too, must be a free decision made possible by a prevenient grace.[29] This freedom is to be understood as a renewal of the will by which we are enabled to obey the divine commandment; it is not the anarchic freedom to do as we please (as in much feminism and in naturalistic hedonism).[30] One is not free to enter into marriage or to leave marriage, as feminists contend. One *becomes* free to enter marriage as a lifelong commitment, and one is not free to break one's vows except by a special divine dispensation.[31]

In the area of church activity and church offices, the patriarchalist insists on strict role differentiation between the sexes and bars women from having any administrative or teaching authority over men. The feminist, on the other hand, sees sex as irrelevant in the realizing of tasks in the church and regards with particular disfavor those women who eagerly accept what are considered menial or serving roles (such as kitchen work). The covenantalist position envisions man and woman working in partnership in all areas of church life, under the Lordship of Christ. Though recognizing the place for special working fellowships for men or women in the church (if purely voluntary), it generally discourages sex segregation, seeing as the basis for unity or cohesion in its groups not sex, marital status, or age, but the common commitment to the Christian mission.

The biblical view represents the nullification of the other positions. It challenges patriarchalism by transforming the meaning of headship.[32] It calls romanticism into question by relativizing the experience of romantic love. It sharply contradicts hedonistic naturalism by placing sex in the service of marriage. It takes issue with feminism by emphasizing the dependence of woman on man and the responsibility of woman to her husband and family.

In Sweden, as well as in some other Scandinavian countries, we see the decline of traditional patriarchal values and the ascendancy of a naturalistic hedonism which on occasion maintains an uneasy alliance with radical feminism.[33] The woman's liberation movement is quite vigorous in Sweden, and while it has succeeded in eroding the authority of the husband and father in the family, it has not been able to safeguard the essential dignity of woman. Despite its protestations against rampant pornography and prostitution, it has not been able to stem the tide toward naturalism where woman becomes the object of sexual exploitation.

Christian morality in Sweden is being fiercely challenged by an aggressive neo-paganism. Some have observed a trend toward masculinity in the Swedish woman, evident in the penchant for unisex clothing. Yet one could also point to the sexualization of the Swedish woman where she sees her role as an enticer of man, often taking the initiative in sexual encounters. A woman who chooses the role of a homemaker or home-builder instead of a career outside the home is generally looked upon with contempt. The recent child abuse law in Sweden (passed in July 1979) virtually exempts children from the discipline of the home. There is presently legislation pending that will permit children to divorce their parents and in effect to become wards of the state. Moreover, a serious discipline problem exists in the classroom, so that some women teachers live in constant fear of being molested by sexually precocious students. Instead of fairy tales, many children's books focus on politics, divorce, and unwed mothers. Explicit sex-education manuals are made available for children as young as three years old. The public schools inculcate pagan values which are intended to subvert the Christian moral code. Co-ed showers, which are now the rule in Swedish schools, foster a climate of sexual permissiveness. One third of all pregnancies are terminated by abortion. The majority of marriages in Sweden are neither civil nor religious, and divorce in these cases is simply by common consent. The emphasis on the pursuit of pleasure, coupled with an almost servile dependence on the state for welfare benefits, has contributed to a metaphysical vacuum where people begin to question whether there is any meaning in life. It is not surprising that the suicide rate in Sweden is exceptionally and tragically high. The New Testament recommendation of lifelong celibacy or virginity for the sake of the kingdom is generally not considered a serious option, even in church circles.[34]

I have given attention to what is happening in Sweden because there are trends toward the same moral climate in our own nation. The radical feminist movement is abetting these tendencies despite the fact that woman is destined to end up in a new kind of bondage. The breakdown of the family in our own society is reflected in the disappearance of what Barth calls the biblical principle of superordination and subordination. The woman is no longer subject to the man (in any respect), and children are no longer subject to the discipline of their parents. By demanding absolute control over their own bodies, feminist women are to a high degree responsible for permissive abortion, which can only prepare the way for infanticide.[35]

In opposing militant feminism, however, we must not make the mistake of enthroning patriarchal values that have often held women and children in bondage and oppression. The answer to feminism is not a reversion to an autocratic or narrow patriarchalism as we sometimes find it expressed in a revitalized religious fundamentalism.[36] The answer lies in a reaffirmation of the biblical alternative, which sees male-female relations patterned after the covenant that God made with Israel and that Christ makes with his church.

In this day when every person wishes to do his or her own thing, we need a life- and world-view that stresses the interdependence of man and woman and the subordination of both to the will of God. Man needs woman for companionship and loving support, just as woman needs man for direction and loving care. Even in a patriarchal culture, it has been recognized that behind every successful man is a great woman. Christian faith goes further and affirms that more often than not, behind every man of God there is a holy woman. Behind Jesus there was Mary; behind

Augustine there was Monica; behind Luther there was Katherine von Bora; behind Pascal there was Jacqueline; behind John Wesley there was Susanna Wesley; behind George Fox there was Margaret Fell.

Finally, we must recover the biblical wisdom that man and woman are created for fellowship, that each is incomplete apart from the other. This does not mean that everyone or practically everyone is intended to marry (as patriarchy insists), but it does mean that even those who choose the single life make their choice with a view to working together with members of the opposite sex for the achievement of common tasks. Just as man is deficient apart from woman, so woman cannot be sufficient apart from man. Against the trend toward male and female independency, Christian faith affirms the ideal of partnership in service, with some differentiation in roles but a unity in purpose. As Christian men and women, we need to rediscover and reaffirm our essential equality as heirs in Christ, but at the same time to recognize that we are called to live out our vocations in different ways. Woman cannot be the substitute for man, but she can be the complement of man. Just as Christ loves and serves his church and his church serves him, so the wife must serve her husband and family and the husband must love and provide for his wife.[37] When we begin to see marriage and family in a theocentric and Christocentric perspective, we shall then witness the renewal of marriage and the recovery of family solidarity and unity.

The truly liberated man and woman are those who have been set free not to realize vain ambition but to serve the advancement of the kingdom of God in the world. Having come to know the liberty of the children of God, they have learned, sometimes painfully, that the key to the victorious life lies not in prideful presumption but in loving subordination—to one another and above all to the God who is the Lord and Giver of all life.

Notes

CHAPTER ONE / *The Present Controversy*

1. See Mary Daly, *Beyond God the Father* (Boston: Beacon Press, 1973). In her latest book *Gyn/Ecology: The Metaethics of Radical Feminism* (Boston: Beacon Press, 1979), Daly repudiates androgyny in favor of lesbianism. This book is addressed to the "Lesbian Imagination in All Women."
2. Helen M. Luke, *Woman Earth and Spirit* (New York: Crossroad, 1981). Luke leans heavily on Carl G. Jung.
3. See Thomas D. Parker, *The Reality of God in a Male-Female World,* unpublished paper read at the Midwest Division of the American Theological Society, Bethany Theological Seminary, Oak Brook, Ill., November 1978.
4. A notable exception is Ann Belford Ulanov who seeks to recover the "distinctively feminine modality of being." She wishes to do justice to those traditional capacities for intuition and receptivity that have been attributed to women. See Ann Belford Ulanov, *Receiving Woman: Studies in the Psychology and Theology of the Feminine* (Philadelphia: Westminster Press, 1981). For a feminist retort to Ulanov see Rosemary Ruether's review of this book in *The Christian Century,* Vol. XCVIII, No. 36 (November 11, 1981), pp. 1168-1169.
5. Karl Barth, *Church Dogmatics* III, 4, eds. G. W. Bromiley and T. F. Torrance (Edinburgh: T. & T. Clark, 1961), p. 156.
6. Elisabeth Elliot, *Let Me Be A Woman* (Wheaton: Tyndale House, 1976), p. 59.
7. Along these same lines, in a new book of prayers and hymns published by the British Council of Churches, young people are encouraged to address their prayers to "Parent God." See Jean Caffey Lyles, "The God-Language Bind," *The Christian Century,* Vol. XCVII, No. 14 (April 16, 1980), pp. 430, 431.
8. See *Language About God "Opening the Door"* (New York: Advisory Council on Discipleship and Worship, 1975), p. 6. This document was adopted by the 187th General Assembly of the United Presbyterian Church U.S.A. in May 1975. In a similar vein Ann Plogsterth suggests the neuter term "Divine Providence" as a suitable substitute for masculine metaphors for deity (such as "Heavenly Father") and advocates referring to God by the impersonal

"It." In "Toward a Genderless God," *National Catholic Reporter,* Vol. 16, No. 15 (February 8, 1980), p. 14.

9. Some feminists go further and trace the root of the human malaise to the family and its stress on private property. See Jill Tweedie, *In the Name of Love* (New York: Pantheon, 1979).
10. See Nancy Hardesty, "Toward A Total Human Theology," *Sojourners* 5:5 (May/June, 1976), pp. 35-37; Letty M. Russell, "Women and Ministry," *Sexist Religion and Women in the Church–No More Silence!,* ed. Alice L. Hageman (New York: Association Press, 1974); and Peggy Ann Way, "An Authority of Possibility for Women in the Church," *Women's Liberation and the Church,* ed. Sarah Bentley Doely (New York: Association Press, 1970).
11. See Paul K. Jewett, *Man as Male and Female* (Grand Rapids: Eerdmans, 1975), pp. 111ff.; and Virginia Mollenkott, "A Conversation with Virginia Mollenkott," *The Other Side* (May/June, 1976), pp. 22-28. Jewett sees Paul's overall teaching as normative and differentiates between Paul's rabbinic inheritance and his mature thought.
12. See Nadine Brozan, "In the Religious Life, a Conflict of Faith and Feminism," *New York Times* (March 8, 1980), p. 18. Ware blithely overlooks the fact that her own view is culturally contingent.
13. Against this position Phyllis Trible argues that the Bible does not allow for an androgynous interpretation: "From the beginning humankind exists as two creatures, not as one creature with double sex." In *God and the Rhetoric of Sexuality* (Philadelphia: Fortress, 1978), p. 18. Stephen Clark gives this sound advice: "The wisest approach is not to encourage people to articulate in their lives traits which are typical of the opposite sex, since that leads to masculinization of women and feminization of men. Rather, people should be urged to express common human traits in a way which is characteristic of their sex." In *Man and Woman in Christ* (Ann Arbor, Mich.: Servant Books, 1980), p. 633.
14. Sheila D. Collins, "Toward a Feminist Theology," *The Christian Century,* Vol. LXXXIX, No. 28 (August 2, 1972), p. 799.
15. Matthew Fox, *Whee! We, wee All the Way Home: A Guide to the New Sensual Spirituality* (Wilmington, N.C.: Consortium Books, 1976), p. 95.
16. Daly, *Beyond God the Father,* pp. 124-127. Also see Letha Scanzoni and Virginia R. Mollenkott, *Is the Homosexual My Neighbor?* (New York: Harper & Row, 1978), where a "homosexual Christian ethic" is proposed.
17. See Dale Vree in *National Review,* Vol. XXXI, No. 31 (August 3, 1979), p. 974.
18. R. C. Zaehner, *Our Savage God* (New York: Sheed & Ward, 1974), p. 267.
19. Erich Fromm, *The Crisis of Psychoanalysis* (New York: Holt, Rinehart & Winston, 1970), p. 90.
20. For an in-depth probing of male-female roles in the light of the social sciences see Stephen Clark, *Man and Woman in Christ.* This book is an able defense of an updated and slightly more enlightened patriarchalism which appeals to both the biblical witness and the findings of the social sciences. Clark's patriarchal orientation is evident when he declares that the decision "to have women acting as heads of Christian people" means that "the scriptural vision of the life of humans together is no longer applicable or appropriate"

(p. 656). Despite his very helpful exegesis of difficult scriptural texts and his insightful analysis of the breakdown of the family in modern society, the author can be faulted for not doing justice to those biblical passages that depict women in leadership roles. Moreover, his tendency to see the woman primarily as a helper to man prevents him from doing full justice to the biblical truth that woman was intended to be a companion of man as well. See my review of Clark's book: Donald G. Bloesch, "Traditional Roles Defended," *Christianity Today*, Vol. XXVI, No. 7 (April 24, 1981), p. 56.

21. Cited in *Christianity Today*, Vol. XX, No. 7 (January 2, 1976), p. 24.
22. David Bakan, *And They Took Themselves Wives: The Emergence of Patriarchy in Western Civilization* (San Francisco: Harper & Row, 1979). Whereas Bakan contends that in patriarchy men take a keen interest in their children, Rita Gross in critiquing Bakan's book raises the disturbing question whether in patriarchy men are really "interested in their own *biological fatherhood* and in the continuity of their own physiological line, in which case children become the means to that end." See Rita M. Gross, "Taking an Interest," *The Christian Century*, Vol. XCVIII, No. 11 (April 1, 1981), pp. 362, 363.
23. For a succinct traditionalist statement of Christian patriarchalism see Larry Christenson, *The Christian Family* (Minneapolis: Bethany Fellowship, 1970) and Larry and Nordis Christenson, *The Christian Couple* (Minneapolis: Bethany Fellowship, 1977). While there is a certain amount of biblical wisdom in these books, they contain an authoritarian thrust that smacks more of the Victorian than the biblical heritage. Headship is interpreted as "exercising authority over," and the use of the rod upon children is advocated as the first and not the last response of parents to any challenge to their authority. Nothing is said of the growing practice of child abuse in the home. The patriarchal bias is also evident in the authors' opposition to all forms of contraception, thereby implying that marriage should be seen as basically in the service of reproduction. Yet they also acknowledge that authority must be exercised in humility and that "submission" does not mean "servility."
24. For an insightful exposition of Barth's understanding of subordination in male-female relations, see A. J. McKelway, "The Concept of Subordination in Barth's Special Ethics," *Scottish Journal of Theology*, Vol. 32, No. 4 (1979), pp. 345-357. For Barth, the leadership expected of the man must not transgress the limit God has set for him in relation to the woman; nor can it threaten her freedom and autonomy or deny the love that each owes the other. In this view, disobedience to the divine order is conspicuous in both the compliant woman and the overaggressive man as well as in their opposites.
25. Reinhold Niebuhr, *The Nature and Destiny of Man*, Vol. I (New York: Charles Scribner's Sons, 1951), p. 282.
26. This is by no means to insinuate, as some feminists do, that a woman cannot realize her vocation under God in being a homemaker and mother; but when this becomes a law rather than a free decision, we have a situation of oppression.
27. Dietrich Bonhoeffer, *Life Together*, trans. John W. Doberstein (New York: Harper, 1954), pp. 21-26.

CHAPTER TWO / *The Man-Woman Relationship in the Bible*

1. It is man who is given the prerogative of naming both woman and the animals (Gen. 2:20, 23).
2. The Old Testament warns against the enslaving ways of harlots, but at least in the early period of Israelite history whatever sin might be involved was at worst venial. Cult prostitution received a much harsher condemnation. See William Graham Cole, *Sex and Love in the Bible* (New York: Association Press, 1959), pp. 240ff. There was a tendency in Old Testament history to restrict or eliminate the practice of prostitution as far as Israelite girls were concerned. See O. J. Baab, "Prostitution," *The Interpreter's Dictionary of the Bible* (Nashville: Abingdon Press, 1962), pp. 931-934.
3. Barth interestingly maintains that the command to beget children belongs to the old dispensation, since entrance into the kingdom and fruitfulness are reconceived in the New Testament as spiritual realities. Procreation formed an integral part of the spiritual mission of Israel, because the promised Messiah would be a physical descendant of Abraham. Once the Messiah appeared, however, the spiritual necessity for procreation ended. See Karl Barth, *Church Dogmatics,* III, 2, eds. G. W. Bromiley and T. F. Torrance (Edinburgh: T. & T. Clark, 1960), pp. 579-587.
4. The daughter who is sold becomes a concubine who still possesses certain rights. The Hebrews tried to humanize and regulate slavery. The fact that slaves were circumcised and participated in family worship made them brothers and sisters in the faith.
5. On the basis of these passages, Barth sees the special glory of the woman in the fact that she completes the human being. "Without the existence of this helpmeet," he writes, "his [man's] own creation would really not have been complete," *Church Dogmatics,* III, 1, p. 305. Woman's place in creation indicates not her superiority to man, but her excellence as his partner.
6. Paul affirms the duty of children to obey their parents, but he qualifies this by the words "in the Lord" (cf. Eph. 6:1; Col. 3:20). I do not agree with Larry Christenson that children must even obey when their parents command that which is definitely wrong. See his *The Christian Family* (Minneapolis: Bethany Fellowship, 1970), pp. 57ff. It should be noted that Jesus placed fidelity to his messianic vocation over obedience to his parents (cf. Luke 2:41-51; 8:19-21; 14:26).
7. Louis Bouyer sees the woman clothed with the sun in Rev. 12 as the second Eve who thwarts the plans of the devil against humankind. Louis Bouyer, *The Seat of Wisdom,* trans. A. V. Littledale (New York: Pantheon Books, 1962), p. 41.
8. Robin Scroggs, "Woman in the NT," *The Interpreter's Dictionary of the Bible,* Supplementary Volume (Nashville: Abingdon, 1976), p. 967.
9. For an able defense of Paul, showing that his attitude toward women was both advanced and exemplary, see Richard and Joyce Boldrey, *Chauvinist or Feminist?* (Grand Rapids: Baker Book House, 1976).
10. Berkeley and Alvera Mickelsen argue that *kephale* in the Pauline epistles really means exalted originator and completer, source or base, enabler or

source of life. Its essential meaning is not "having authority over" or being of superior rank. "As Christ is the enabler (the one who brings to completion) of the church, so the husband is to enable (bring to completion) all that his wife is meant to be. The husband is to nourish and cherish his wife as he does his own body, even as Christ nourishes and cherishes the church" (Eph. 5:29). Berkeley and Alvera Mickelsen, "The 'Head' of the Epistles," *Christianity Today,* Vol. XXV, No. 4 (February 20, 1981), pp. 20-23. In my opinion, while there is much truth in what they say, these other meanings do not abrogate the idea of directive headship, but instead transform the patriarchal meaning into something more in keeping with the biblical witness to the reconciling act of God in Jesus Christ. The parallel between Christ as Lord of the church and the role of the husband in the family must not be pressed too far, since there is no identity of roles, but nonetheless it provides the key to the overthrow of autocratic patriarchy in the home and the church. My position on this subject is remarkably close to that of James Hurley, who speaks of "the self-sacrificing headship of the husband" and contends that "biblical headship and authority are for the sake of building up others." See James B. Hurley, *Man and Woman in Biblical Perspective* (Leicester, England: InterVarsity Press, 1981), pp. 240, 244.

11. One can also say that the subordination of woman to man in the context of Christian marriage means the exaltation of woman. In biblical thought, it is the lowly, those who are in subjection, who are exalted (cf. Luke 1:47, 48, 52, 53; James 1:9-11). Just as the church as the elect community is raised up by Christ and exalted in Christ, so woman is raised up by man and exalted in and with man. It can even be said that on occasion woman is exalted over man, particularly where man is an oppressor rather than a provider and protector. The man who exalts himself over the woman will be humbled, whereas the woman who humbles herself will be exalted (cf. Matt. 23:11, 12). The husband, too, can only realize his vocation to holiness through humbling himself, giving up the desire always to have his own way (cf. 1 Cor. 13:5). Moreover, just as the Christian who suffers with his Lord will reign with him (2 Tim. 2:12; Rev. 20:6), so the woman who suffers with her husband will likewise reign with him.
12. Barth, *Church Dogmatics,* III, 4, p. 172.
13. C. S. Lewis, *The Four Loves* (New York: Harcourt, Brace & World, 1960), pp. 147-149. Lewis says: "The chrism of this terrible coronation is to be seen not in the joys of any man's marriage but in its sorrows, in the sickness and sufferings of a good wife or the faults of a bad one, in his unwearying (never paraded) care or his inexhaustible forgiveness: forgiveness, not acquiescence" (p. 148).
14. Barth, *Church Dogmatics,* III, 2, pp. 309-316.
15. Some scholars consider the custom of veiling as distinctly oriental and hold that Paul was trying to impose a custom that had its roots in oriental and especially Jewish sensibility. Others contend that veiling was not uncommon among Greek women (though it was not compulsory), but that common prostitutes were always unveiled. In my opinion, the best single analysis of the custom of veiling in the context of Paul's admonitions is found in Hans Conzelmann, *I Corinthians,* trans. James W. Leitch, ed. George W.

MacRae (Philadelphia: Fortress Press, 1975), pp. 181-191. Conzelmann recognizes that it is impossible to state the Greek custom on this matter unequivocally (unlike the Jewish), but indicates that "it can be assumed that respectable Greek women wore a head covering in public" (p. 185). James Hurley (*Man and Woman in Biblical Perspective*) suggests that Paul's principal concern was not veiling, but that women should continue to wear their hair in the distinctive fashion of women—that is—put up, rather than shorn or hanging loose (pp. 168-171). He says it seems "likely that Hebrew customs, as reflected in the Old Testament, were quite close to those of Greece and Rome in the time of Christ and that a woman's hair was a sign of her dignity and honour. A veil might perhaps reemphasize this" (p. 263).

16. Jerome Murphy-O'Connor makes a convincing case that Paul was being evenhanded in his admonitions to the Corinthians in 1 Corinthians 11. He criticizes men who wear long hair as well as women who reject the veil on the grounds that both are blurring the distinctions between the sexes. While affirming the equality of the sexes, Paul is at the same time adamant in maintaining distinctions (which enthusiasts and Gnostics sought to deny). "If there was no longer any male or female, the Corinthians felt free to blur the distinction between the sexes. Unmasculine and unfeminine hairdos flew in the face of accepted conventions in precisely the same way as their approval of incest. Scandal was the symbol of their new spiritual freedom; the more people they shocked, the more right they felt themselves to be." Murphy-O'Connor says that it is misleading to call Paul a patriarchalist, since he broke decisively with patriarchalism in seeing women as charismatic leaders. See his "Sex and Logic in I Corinthians 11:2-16," *The Catholic Biblical Quarterly,* Vol. 42, No. 4 (October 1980), p. 490.
17. For an illuminating study of how Paul transcends his patriarchal background and milieu, see Richard and Catherine Clark Kroeger, "Sexual Identity in Corinth: Paul Faces a Crisis," *The Reformed Journal,* Vol. 28, No. 12 (December 1978), pp. 11-15. This essay has helped me see that in the area of male-female relationships, Paul was a bold innovator. Supportive of this general position is Victor Paul Furnish's *The Moral Teaching of Paul* (Nashville: Abingdon Press, 1979). Furnish contends that Paul's position sharply contradicted the benevolent patriarchy of which he is so often accused.
18. Neither did he deny the difference in the office of elder and deacon (Phil. 1:1; 1 Tim. 3), which had its origin in the apostolic council at Jerusalem (Acts 6:1-6).
19. It is interesting to note that celibacy (as well as virginity) is also regarded with disfavor by the radical feminists, since it signifies the denial of womanly potential and, in the case of those who embrace the conventual life, submission to the male-dominated church. Feminists such as Kate Millett and Germaine Greer contend that the ideal of feminism is sexual freedom and that the life of the woman who approaches this ideal will resemble "compulsive promiscuity," though it will be "fundamentally different." See Germaine Greer, *The Female Eunuch* (New York: McGraw-Hill Co., 1971), pp. 142, 143.
20. L. S. Thornton, *Revelation and the Modern World* (London: A. & C. Black, 1950), p. 12.

21. Karl Barth, *Church Dogmatics,* III, 1, p. 309.
22. This does not imply that one must always be in the physical presence of the opposite sex.
23. According to Phyllis Trible, in the regulations of Ezra a concern for racial, ritual, and sexual purity undercut a respect for woman as a human being. She contends that woman came to be seen as an impure, subordinate, and inferior being. See Phyllis Trible, "Woman in the OT," *The Interpreter's Dictionary of the Bible,* Supplementary Volume, p. 966. Against Trible it can be argued that Ezra's warning was not directed against women as such, but against the danger of marriage to foreign women who might well lead the men of the Jewish nation away from the true faith.
24. See John H. Otwell, *And Sarah Laughed: The Status of Woman in the Old Testament* (Philadelphia: Westminster Press, 1977). Otwell challenges those scholars, a majority, who accept the traditional view of the subordination of women in the patriarchal society of the Old Testament. According to Otwell, a woman's status in the Old Testament is determined ultimately by her relationship to God.
25. According to Austin Stouffer, most people wrongly assume that Paul's emphasis in verse 11 of 1 Timothy 2 is on silence and submission, whereas actually he is emphatically commanding that women be taught. The quietness and full submission that he requires of the woman is what any teacher would ask of his pupils. Paul is not barring women unconditionally from teaching, but instead is making clear that their present need is for instruction in sound doctrine. Stouffer says: "A legitimate rendering of 1 Timothy 2:11-12 thus would be: 'I command that women learn [be taught] in quietness and full submission [to the teaching authority]' (v. 11). 'I am [presently] not permitting a woman to teach and she is not to exert evil influence over a man' (v. 12)." Austin Stouffer, "The Ordination of Women: Yes," *Christianity Today,* Vol. XXV, No. 4 (February 20, 1981), p. 14.
26. This may well indicate that 1 Timothy is a work of a second-generation writer, as a growing body of scholars now hold. If we take such a position, we do not necessarily thereby deny the inspiration of this epistle by the Holy Spirit, nor do we call into question its apostolic authority. It can be argued that the epistle still has its basis in Pauline theology, since the author undoubtedly spoke out of intimate knowledge of the apostle and possibly had in his possession notes of actual conversations. Several scholars who hold to the critical view surmise that the pastoral epistles contain some genuinely Pauline fragments.
27. In Revelation 14:4, virginity is a metaphor that is used to characterize the whole Christian community, since all Christians should be involved in wholehearted and lifelong dedication to Christ. At the same time, it reflects the fact that celibacy and virginity were held in high esteem in the later New Testament period.
28. The beauty of woman is celebrated in Song of Songs 4:1, 3-5; Ezek. 16:7, and in Judith 10:20-23.

CHAPTER THREE / *Women Ministers?*

1. Phyllis Trible, "Woman in the OT," *The Interpreter's Dictionary of the Bible,* Supplementary Volume (Nashville: Abingdon, 1976), p. 964.
2. Oesterley maintains that verse 11 is possibly from a song of victory, and he bluntly asserts that "those who *bring glad tidings* are women." W. O. E. Oesterley, *The Psalms,* Vol. 2 (London: SPCK, 1953), p. 324. Similarly Alexander Maclaren says that it is "the maidens" who chant victory. Alexander Maclaren, *The Psalms,* Vol. 2 (New York: A. C. Armstrong & Son, 1893), p. 278. Some scholars maintain that the "host" or "company" in verse 11 may refer to angels or stars personified as heavenly beings. Here, as in some other cases, a masculine bias in the translating of Scripture prevents us from grasping the original meaning of the text or passage.
3. The passage indicates that Jesus' revelation of himself to the Samaritan woman was designed to bring the gospel to the Samaritans even before it took root among the Jews. With the Samaritan converts who were on their way to see him in mind, Jesus told his disciples, "Lift up your eyes, and see how the fields are already white for harvest" (John 4:35).
4. This does not indicate that women were necessarily numbered among the apostles, but it does suggest that Paul does not exclude the principle of feminine leadership in the churches.
5. Some ancient commentators believed Andronicus and Junia to be a married couple. It should be noted that "Junias" is not found elsewhere in Greek literature and that from a purely lexical point of view the name may very well be "Junia." The editor of *Christianity Today* makes this significant comment: "The King James Version correctly notes the feminine Junia in Romans 16:7 in contrast with most contemporary translations that with little or no justification transform . . . the woman Junia into the man 'Junias' to avoid the unthinkable—a woman among the apostles!' " Vol. XXIII, No. 23 (October 5, 1979), p. 29. John Chrysostom suggests that Junia was given the honorary title of "apostle" because of some special merit (*Homily on Romans* XXXI, *Patrologia Graeca,* ed. J. P. Migne, 60, 670).
6. It is well to note that in Romans 16:1, 2 Paul refers to Phoebe not just as a *diakonos* but as a *prostatis pollōn* (protectress or helper of many). One interpreter comments that "if it were addressed to man," it would probably be translated "ruler of many." See Austin H. Stouffer, "The Ordination of Women: Yes," *Christianity Today,* Vol. XXV, No. 4 (February 20, 1981), p. 15.
7. See Joan Morris, *Against Nature and God* (London: Mowbrays, 1973), p. 119.
8. Commentators are divided on whether Paul is speaking of deaconesses or deacons' wives who share in their husbands' ministry. Elsewhere Paul acknowledges that women shared in the work of deacons (Rom. 16:1).
9. Elisabeth M. Tetlow, "Women in Ministry: A New Testament Perspective," *America,* Vol. 142, No. 7 (February 23, 1980), p. 140. While acknowledging that 1 Timothy forbids women to "teach" or "instruct" in the public

assembly, Tetlow contends that this is a later epistle signifying a deviation from authentic Pauline teaching. In my view, 1 Timothy still has apostolic or canonical authority, though it reflects a different religious situation than that which existed in Corinth in an earlier period.

10. See Richard and Joyce Boldrey, *Chauvinist or Feminist?* (Grand Rapids: Baker Book House, 1976), p. 21.
11. It is interesting to note that Priscilla's name precedes that of her husband four of the six times it is mentioned in the New Testament, and most scholars agree that she was his intellectual superior.
12. See Tertullian, *On Baptism,* XVII. Tertullian opposed women in positions of authority over men.
13. Alexander Souter, ed., *Pelagius's Expositions of Thirteen Epistles of St. Paul,* Vol. 2 (Cambridge: University Press, 1926), p. 211 (on 1 Cor. 14).
14. Thomas Aquinas, *Summa Theologica* I, 92, I c.
15. See Joan Morris, *The Lady Was a Bishop* (New York: Macmillan, 1973).
16. The Renaissance philosopher Jean Bodin (sixteenth century) says in his *De Republica* that women ought to be removed as much as possible from the majesty of government because the rule of woman is contrary to the laws of nature. Montaigne likewise disparaged the rule of women.
17. Cited in Edith Simon, *The Saints* (New York: Dell Publishing Co., 1968), p. 103.
18. Nevertheless, there are passages in the writings of the Reformers that acknowledge the dignity and even the apostolic role of women. John Calvin could make this surprising and welcome observation: "Now though the Apostle John did not depart from the cross, yet no mention is made of him; but praise is bestowed on *the women* alone, who accompanied Christ till death, because their extraordinary attachment to their Master was the more strikingly displayed, when the men fled trembling. . . . Accordingly, when they [the apostles] afterwards proclaimed the gospel, they must have borrowed from *women* the chief portion of the history." John Calvin, *Commentary on a Harmony of the Evangelists, Matthew, Mark, and Luke,* III, trans. William Pringle (Grand Rapids: Baker Book House, 1979 reprint), pp. 328, 329.
19. Cited in Rachel Conrad Wahlberg, "Jesus and the Uterus Image," *Theology Today,* Vol. XXXI, No. 3 (October 1974), p. 229.
20. One interpreter observes: "Puritan women were figures of unquestioned worth and importance, partners with their husbands in the economy of the farm and in the redemption of Christendom." Page Smith, *Daughters of the Promised Land: Women in American History* (Boston: Little, Brown, 1970), pp. 55, 56.
21. See Friedhelm Rudersdorf, *Dora Rappard: Die Mutter von St. Chrischona* (Giessen and Basel: Brunnen-Verlag, 1956). While her husband was the official director of the mission, Dora Rappard played a significant leadership role in the life of the community as well as in the wider evangelical revival movement.
22. See Lucille Sider Dayton and Donald W. Dayton, " 'Your Daughters Shall Prophesy': Feminism in the Holiness Movement," *Methodist History,* Vol. XIV, No. 2 (January 1976), pp. 67-92. For a helpful overall view of the

ministry of women in the church through the ages, with special emphasis on the modern scene, see Nancy Hardesty, *Great Women of Faith* (Grand Rapids: Baker, 1980).

23. Karl Stern, *The Flight From Woman* (New York: Farrar, Straus & Giroux, 1965), p. 161.
24. It can be argued that a woman minister who seeks to remain fully feminine can better exemplify the total dependence on the Word demanded of all Christians than a man who in asserting his masculinity is tempted to lord it over the Word.
25. Jürgen Fangmeier and Hinricht Stoevesandt, eds. *Karl Barth Letters 1961-1968,* trans. & ed. Geoffrey W. Bromiley (Grand Rapids: Eerdmans, 1981), p. 279.
26. A team ministry may not necessarily be in keeping with God's purposes, since there is a surprisingly high rate of divorce among clergy couples, particularly in the mainline denominations. One possible explanation is that husband and wife come to be rivals rather than partners in ministry. The rate of divorce among clergy couples in the Salvation Army is very low. For a book that holds out hope for clergy marriages, see David and Vera Mace, *What's Happening to Clergy Marriages?* (Nashville: Abingdon Press, 1980).
27. This is not to suggest that women endowed with exceptional spiritual discernment and wisdom may not also function as counselors to both men and women. But at present when women in ministry are still not fully accepted, male support seems especially valuable.

CHAPTER FOUR / *Revising the Language About God*

1. Speaking out of a feminist perspective, Carol Christ contends that both moderate and radical feminism "challenge the core symbolism of both Judaism and Christianity" and that this challenge must be taken with the utmost seriousness. Carol P. Christ, "The New Feminist Theology: A Review of the Literature," *Religious Studies Review,* Vol. 3, No. 4 (October 1977), p. 203. Patricia Wilson-Kastner, who takes issue with revolutionary feminists, nonetheless holds that "basic changes" are necessary in Christianity's self-understanding in order to meet the challenge of the feminist movement. Patricia Wilson-Kastner, "Christianity and New Feminist Religions." In *The Christian Century* Vol. XCVIII, No. 27 (Sept. 9, 1981), pp. 864-868.
2. Another alteration in hymnody advocated by some feminists is substituting "Praise, My Soul, the *Queen* of Heaven" for "Praise, My Soul, the *King* of Heaven" (italics mine). But because "queen" tends to imply the existence of a "king" (the first meaning of "queen" is "wife or consort of a king," *Random House Dictionary*), and because of the ineradicable pagan overtones of the appellation "Queen of Heaven" (it was historically associated with various pagan religions as well as Christian heresies), it would seem that in adopting this language we have moved from a strict monotheism into the thought-world of polytheism. In Catholic circles, the term "Queen of Heaven" might imply the elevation of Mary into the Godhead, thereby supplanting the Trinity with a Quaternity, though this is not the intention of Catholic theologians who use this language. Nonetheless, in Catholic popu-

lar devotion the appellation "Queen of Heaven" in reference to Mary often connotes divinity.

An incisive critique of feminist attempts to rewrite hymns and prayers is given by Erik Routley in his "Sexist Language: A View From a Distance," *Worship*, Vol. 53, No. 1 (January 1979), pp. 2-11. Routley's recommendations are sound and helpful. While he allows for changes in language pertaining to human beings, he is adamant that the language about God cannot be altered without severing ties to Christian tradition. He argues that the intuitions of laypeople in this area are more to be trusted than the opinions of self-styled experts.

3. A task-force report to the National Council of Churches released in June, 1980 recommends that Christ be called the "Child of God," not the Son. It also suggests that we should refrain from referring to God with pronouns. See *Newsweek*, Vol. XCV, No. 25 (June 23, 1980), p. 87; and *The Christian Century*, Vol. XCVII, No. 23 (July 2-9, 1980), p. 696.
4. Matthew Fox declares: "The liberation of God from stale, stifling, hierarchical categories of maleness is a spiritual liberation for God herself." In his *Whee! We, wee All the Way Home: A Guide to the New Sensual Spirituality* (Wilmington, N.C.: Consortium Books, 1976), p. 96.
5. Dorothee Sölle, *Death by Bread Alone*, trans. David L. Scheidt (Philadelphia: Fortress Press, 1978), pp. 85, 91. Also see Dorothee Sölle, "Mysticism, Liberation and the Names of God." In *Christianity and Crisis*, Vol. 41, No. 11 (June 22, 1981), pp. 179-185.
6. Carol Ochs, *Behind the Sex of God* (Boston: Beacon Press, 1977), p. 137.
7. Goldenberg is out of sympathy with those who expend their energies in revising the language of the biblical tradition. She astutely perceives that attempts by some of her feminist colleagues to alter the language about God in the Bible and church liturgy may well represent a yearning if not an active seeking for new gods and new myths that stand at variance with biblical religion. See Naomi R. Goldenberg, *Changing of the Gods* (Boston: Beacon Press, 1979), pp. 10-25.
8. Deborah H. Barackman, "Evangelical Women's Caucus: Journeyings," *Eternity*, Vol. 31, No. 11 (December 1980), p. 35. An in-depth and perspicacious critique of evangelical feminism is given by Susan T. Foh in her *Women and the Word of God* (Grand Rapids: Baker Book House, 1981). Although some of her conclusions are debatable, she is to be commended for her serious and thorough treatment of biblical texts, based on a deep respect for the Bible as the Word of God.
9. For an able defense of the biblical view as opposed to process philosophy, see Colin Gunton, *Becoming and Being* (New York: Oxford University Press, 1978).
10. A certain kind of feminism, particularly that which is attracted to the ancient religion of witchcraft, would be open to polytheism and metaphysical pluralism as well as to metaphysical monism. A feminism purified and reformed in the light of God's self-revelation in Jesus Christ as attested in Scripture would find its spiritual home in biblical theism. On the affinities between feminism and process philosophy, see Sheila Greeve Davaney, ed., *Feminism and Process Thought* (New York and Toronto: Edwin Mellen Press, 1981).

11. This does not mean that there is a separate feminine principle in God (analogous to Plato's "receptacle"), but that femininity as well as masculinity has its basis in God. It also means that God can be described by metaphors of gender, since he is authentically personal and not impersonal or suprapersonal.
12. The books of the Apocrypha in the intertestamental period do not have canonical authority for Protestants, but they are helpful in elucidating themes already present in Scripture. It is well to be reminded that Luther often used the Apocrypha as a confirmatory aid. The Lutheran, Zurich Reformed, and Anglican churches have acknowledged the usefulness of the Apocrypha without recognizing its full canonicity.
13. According to Bouyer, Sirach identifies Wisdom both with the original creative Word and with the personal presence of God in Zion. See Louis Bouyer, *The Seat of Wisdom,* trans. Fr. A. V. Littledale (New York: Pantheon Books, 1962), p. 25.
14. Susan Foh makes a pertinent point that the feminine similes and metaphors used to describe God in the Bible do not have the same force as the masculine analogies. Whereas God describes himself as Father, he is only likened indirectly to a mother. A verse often appealed to by feminists is Deuteronomy 32:18: "You were unmindful of the Rock that begot you, and you forgot the God who gave you birth." Foh makes this astute comment: "In this verse, the maternal and paternal responsibility for Israel's birth is said to be God's. The point is that God alone is their progenitor. At first glance, this verse seems to be ideal for those who advocate the Motherhood of God. However, the maternal verb is a *masculine* singular participle; all adjectives, verb forms, and pronouns that refer to God in the Old Testament are masculine. The fatherhood analogy is definitely and overwhelmingly the controlling analogy." She goes on to remind us that Jesus always referred to God as Father and that the parable of the woman with the lost coin (Luke 15:8-10) is no exception: "The point of the parable concerns God's relationship to the lost sinner, not the gender of God." Susan T. Foh, *Women and the Word of God: A Response to Biblical Feminism,* pp. 152, 153. Foh's concern to uphold traditional language concerning God prevents her from doing full justice to the feminine dimension in the being and activity of God.
15. Elaine H. Pagels, "What Became of God the Mother?" in Carol P. Christ and Judith Plaskow, eds., *Womanspirit Rising* (San Francisco: Harper & Row, 1979), p. 107. See also Elaine Pagels, *The Gnostic Gospels* (New York: Random House, 1979). It is significant that in the Hebrew language there was not even a word for "goddess."
16. Pagels acknowledges that Clement of Alexandria is an exception to the orthodox pattern of viewing God as exclusively masculine, but she suggests that Clement may have been influenced by Gnostic teaching (*The Gnostic Gospels,* pp. 67, 68). My position is that Clement was basically orthodox in his doctrine of God and in his Christology, but that he sought to rediscover the feminine dimension of the sacred, partly in order to enhance the credibility of orthodox Christianity in its conflict with Gnosticism. Clement, to his credit, also affirmed the active participation of women in the community of faith, even allowing them leadership roles. It should be noted that feminine

metaphors pertaining to God are more apparent in the language of devotion than in speculative theology among the fathers and mystics of the Catholic church.

17. Karl Barth, *Church Dogmatics,* IV, 1, eds. G. W. Bromiley & T. F. Torrance (Edinburgh: T. & T. Clark, 1956), p. 195.
18. It is my position that as a general rule the Spirit should be described as feminine only indirectly—that is, in his veiled presence as the soul of the church; for this, indeed, is the biblical pattern. The Spirit who acts upon humanity with transforming power is properly designated as masculine, but in his role as receiver of the divine initiative in and through the actions of believing humanity (the church) he can be thought of as feminine. To refer to the Spirit *directly* or *primarily* as feminine is to open the door to an immanentalist concept of deity. One can say that God in his *manifest* presence is normally to be designated by masculine and hierarchical symbols, because this is the biblical pattern. God in his *hidden* presence in the church may be envisioned as feminine, but feminine symbolism is to be applied (as a general rule) not to God himself, but to the church as the spiritual mother of the faithful, the body of Christ, and the bearer of the Spirit. This, too, is the biblical pattern.
19. To refer to the church as mother is also indirectly to refer to the motherhood of the Spirit of God, who is the soul of the church.
20. We may sing praises to the church both as a holy creation of God and as the mystical body of Christ. Many hymns, both Catholic and Protestant, contain such words of praise, as do several of the Psalms. See especially the following hymns: "O Church of God, Triumphant," "Glorious Things of Thee Are Spoken," and "Jerusalem the Golden." The latter, written by Bernard of Cluny, speaks of the church triumphant in the following way: "Who art, with God the Father/ And Spirit, ever blest!" No. 606 in *The Covenant Hymnal* (Chicago: Covenant Press, 1973).
21. Similarly, the fourth-century orthodox Christian father Aphraates could describe the Holy Spirit as the "mother" of humanity, even while referring to God as the "father." See Leonard Swidler, *Biblical Affirmations of Woman* (Philadelphia: Westminster Press, 1979), p. 60. In the Scriptures, the Hebrew *ruach* is feminine, whereas the Greek *pneuma* is neuter. Yet "the Holy Spirit" in the New Testament is increasingly thought of in personal terms, as the living God in action, as "he" rather than "it." The church, which signifies the presence of the Spirit indirectly, is consistently portrayed as feminine. The close relation of the Spirit and the church is evident in 1 Cor. 3:16; 12:13; Phil. 3:3; Eph. 2:21, 22; 4:3; Rev. 22:17.
22. In his role as begetter of spiritual children for Christ, the Spirit is rightly depicted as masculine, for he plants the seed of the new birth within the elect of God. But in his role in leading people to accept the gift of the new life in Christ and in his role in nurturing this gift, he can be thought of as feminine. The Spirit both fathers children and brings children to birth (as a mother).
23. Cf. Sirach 4:11: "Wisdom raises her sons to greatness and cares for those who seek her" (NEB) (cf. Luke 7:35). For a fascinating analysis of the expression and repression of *Sophia* (Wisdom) in Judaeo-Christian faith, see Joan Chamberlain Engelsman, *The Feminine Dimension of the Divine* (Phila-

delphia: Westminster Press, 1979). Unfortunately, like many feminists today, she holds that moral evil must be predicated of God (just as moral contraries were mixed in the goddesses of the pagan mystery religions).

Since Wisdom is closely associated with Providence in the Wisdom Literature (cf. Wis. of Sol. 8:1; 11:20; Prov. 8:15, 16), Providence itself may in the right context be designated by feminine metaphors. It is well to note that both the Greek and Latin roots of Providence are feminine. In Wisdom of Solomon 14:3, Providence is distinguished from God the Father and yet is given divine qualities. In later theology, Providence was related to the preservative work of the Spirit. In my opinion, it is etymologically and theologically proper to refer to Providence (as the personification of God) with feminine pronouns and adjectives, at least on occasion. (The neuter designation has been much more common in Christian history, and there is a theological rationale for this as well.) In this concept of Providence, the feminine can be seen to be hidden and contained in the masculine, just as the masculine is revealed through the feminine.

24. Augustine at least once used the phrase, "Our Mother, the Wisdom of God," *Questionum Evangeliorum,* 1:36. Migne, *Patrologia Latina* 35, col. 1330. For further patristic allusions to divine maternity, see Ritamary Bradley in *Christian Scholar's Review,* Vol. 8, No. 2 (1978), pp. 101-113.

25. In relationship to the Father, both the Son and the Spirit may be thought of as feminine as well as masculine; but in relationship to us they should generally be designated as masculine, since we as the people of God then assume the role of the feminine in receiving the divine initiative. We do not possess God, but we are possessed by God. Christ is the bridegroom, and we are his bride, the church. This should be a general rule but not a law, since there may possibly be occasions for addressing the Word of God in his role as Wisdom as "mother" or even "sister," particularly in private devotions.

26. See Louis Bouyer, *The Seat of Wisdom,* pp. 131-157. Bouyer is emphatic that the maternal relation can find no place in God himself because motherhood implies not the first and sovereign source of creativity, but a reflex activity (p. 148). Yet he does acknowledge that the designation of Wisdom as mother of the faithful originally applied to Christ, not to Mary (pp. 20-28).

27. A distinction should always be maintained between the symbols used for God in public worship and those used in private devotions. What is appropriate in the former may not be necessary in the latter, though it should be normative for the latter. We also need to distinguish between primary and secondary use in the language about God. Both Augustine and Aquinas could refer to Wisdom as our Mother, but this was definitely subordinate to their primary designation of God as Father.

28. Nestorianism saw the two natures of Christ as only loosely associated rather than organically related and inseparable. Feminists who separate Christ and Jesus, referring to the former by feminine adjectives and pronouns and the latter by masculine, have only a Logos *asarkos* (outside the flesh), not a Logos *ensarkos* (incarnate in flesh). John Cobb, who opposes neuterization in our language about God, declares: "The Logos is indissolubly bound up with Christ, and because Jesus was Christ, Christ must be referred to as 'he.' " In his *Christ in a Pluralistic Age* (Philadelphia: Westminster, 1975), p.

263. Cobb, however, rejects the title "Father" for naming the unity of God, preferring instead "Whitehead's vision" in which "the 'feminine' aspect of God . . . is final, inclusive, and fully actual" (p. 264).

29. Other parallels between the German Christian movement and radical feminism can be noted. Both movements appeal to present-day cultural experience over Scripture and therefore represent natural rather than biblical theology; both reinterpret God in mystical, pantheistic terms—as beyond personality; both tend to separate the eternal Christ-Spirit from the historical Jesus; and both seek to draw upon pre-Christian forms of religion.

30. This is not to deny that the church in its human side also plays a part in the new birth, but here its role is instrumental and ministerial in that it ministers to the work of the Holy Spirit. The invisible church, the mystical body of Christ, neither receives nor conveys the grace of salvation except through the instrumentality of the visible church.

31. Because the divinity of the church is hidden in its visible or outward form and is not to be identified with this form, the church in and of itself should not be referred to as our *divine mother*. It is the bearer of the divine, but not the divine itself. The church is more properly described as our *holy mother* who reflects and attests the motherhood of God.

    It should be noted that both Calvin and Luther, in contrast to Barth, had no hesitation in referring to the church as our "holy mother" who bears, nourishes and brings up children for God. For Calvin's views, see John Calvin, *Institutes of the Christian Religion* Vol. II, Bk. IV, Ch. I, 1-4, edited by John T. McNeill, trans. Ford Lewis Battles (Philadelphia: Westminster Press, 1960), pp. 1011-1016.

32. For an illuminating treatment of the biblical significance of Mary, including her divine motherhood, by a Reformed theologian, see Max Thurian, *Mary, Mother of All Christians,* trans. Neville B. Cryer (New York: Herder & Herder, 1964). Thurian declares: "The divine motherhood of Mary is a truly human motherhood in the deep sense of the unity of mother and son, the human mother of God and the Son of God made man" (pp. 72, 73).

33. When as evangelical Christians we refer to our "mother in heaven," we should have in mind first of all the church triumphant (cf. Gal. 4:26) and then St. Mary, who with the other saints in glory intercedes for the church on earth. Luther describes Mary thus: "It was always possible for her to fall, but she is the eternal dwelling-place of the Holy Spirit, and she remains perpetually holy, and blessed Mother for eternity." *D. Martin Luthers Werke* (Weimarer Ausgabe, 1883ff.), 37:97, 11 to 13.

34. The Eastern Orthodox theologian John Meyendorff declares: "There is no doubt in my mind that the Protestant rejection of the veneration of Mary and its various consequences . . . is one of the *psychological* reasons which explains the recent emergence of institutional feminism." Cited in Peter Moore, ed., *Man, Woman, and Priesthood* (London: SPCK, 1978), p. 78. Meyendorff's statement does not explain why many Catholic women have been attracted to ideological feminism.

35. Harry Blamires, *The Faith and Modern Error* (London: SPCK, 1964), p. 76.

36. See Paul Tillich, *The Interpretation of History,* trans. N. A. Rasetzki and Elsa L. Talmey (New York: Charles Scribner's Sons, 1936), pp. 46, 47; and his *The Shaking of the Foundations* (New York: Charles Scribner's Sons, 1948), pp. 153ff.
37. Paul Jewett contends that the word "father" for God is a generic, not a specific, term, in his *Man as Male and Female* (Grand Rapids: Eerdmans, 1975), p. 168. In my view it is both generic and specific, since it is a self-designation and is not merely drawn from the human experience of fatherhood. Yet "fatherhood" when applied to God, even the first person of the Trinity, contains also the element of motherhood, for maternity has its basis in paternity. How else could the Holy Spirit, sometimes portrayed as feminine in the Old Testament, proceed from the Father unless the Father encompassed femininity within himself? That God chooses, through his inspired writers, to describe himself as Father and Lord, however, means that in our preaching and worship we are bound to respect and honor these designations, because they are given for the purpose of worship that is done "in spirit and truth" (John 4:23, 24).
38. It is well to note that in the light of the biblical witness we can say that God is like a mother, but never that God *is* a Mother, because in his relationship to us as Creator and Redeemer God designates himself as Father. Yet in the Bible, the word "Father" in reference to God generally includes such motherly attributes as tenderheartedness and loving care. He is a Father who epitomizes the ideal qualities of human fatherhood, but these also include qualities associated with human motherhood. Because God as heavenly Father is both inclusive and specific, and because this is the biblical way of speaking of God, we can say that the biblical God is primarily Father and that other designations, especially those of a feminine character, are to be seen as secondary, but not insignificant. Similarly, it is theologically proper to assert that God is essentially and primarily transcendent and secondarily immanent. This is to say, he is above us before he is within us and beneath us.
39. Karl Barth, *Church Dogmatics: Index Volume with Aids for the Preacher,* ed. G. W. Bromiley & T. F. Torrance (Edinburgh: T. & T. Clark, 1977), p. 495.
40. Hendrikus Berkhof, *Christian Faith,* trans. Sierd Woudstra (Grand Rapids: Eerdmans, 1979), p. 69.
41. Thomas Aquinas, *Summa Theologica,* I, q. 13, art. 3.
42. It can be argued (as does Benedict Ashley, O.P.) that although Aquinas makes use of the term *analogia entis* or something similar, his actual method is the analogy of faith, since he begins his *Summa Theologica* with divine revelation and then seeks to use analogy to make the truth of revelation intelligible. (Guest lecture in my theology class at Aquinas Institute of Theology, Dubuque, Iowa, April 8, 1975.) Bromiley perhaps goes too far in calling Thomas a theologian of revelation alone, not of reason and revelation. Yet I believe Bromiley to be sound in his view that for Thomas, true or saving knowledge of God is possible only on the basis of revelation. Bromiley reminds us that according to Thomas natural knowledge of God is

always mixed with error. Geoffrey W. Bromiley, *Historical Theology, An Introduction* (Grand Rapids: Eerdmans, 1978), pp. 196-209. Von Balthasar sees points of convergence between the Thomistic understanding of analogy and Karl Barth's approach. Hans Urs von Balthasar, *The Theology of Karl Barth,* trans. John Drury (New York: Holt, Rinehart and Winston, 1971), pp. 100ff., 286-288, 295-296. For Von Balthasar, "Barth's way of understanding God's Revelation in Christ (the analogy of faith) includes within itself the analogy of being; in the Catholic Christocentric approach presented here, the analogy of being becomes concrete and real only within the more all-embracing analogy of faith" (pp. 286-287). In the light of this discussion, one can say that the differences between man and woman are rooted in the order of creation, but that these differences are illumined by the analogy of faith.

43. It must nonetheless be recognized that Jesus Christ remained Lord even in his role as servant. He exercised dominion and authority even in his humiliation. This means that he still demands from us our worship and allegiance.
44. Moltmann, who conceives of God as "Fatherly-Motherly Spirit" rather than majestic Lord, radically reinterprets the doctrine of creation: "Creation as God's act in Nothingness and as God's order in chaos is a male, an engendering notion. Creation as God's act in God and out of God must rather be called a feminine concept, a bringing forth: God creates the world by letting his world become and be in *himself.*" Rejecting *creatio ex nihilo,* he accepts the idea of emanation in the sense of a divine overflowing. Jürgen Moltmann, *The Trinity and the Kingdom,* trans. Margaret Kohl (San Francisco: Harper & Row, 1981), pp. 109, 113.
45. Kallistos Ware, "Man, Woman, and the Priesthood of Christ," in Peter Moore, ed., *Man, Woman, and Priesthood,* p. 84. Ware reminds us that the symbols that the faith applies to God "are not chosen by us but revealed and *given.*" In his *The Orthodox Way* (Crestwood, New York: St. Vladimir's Orthodox Theological Seminary, 1979), p. 42.
46. Starhawk, *The Spiral Dance: A Rebirth of the Ancient Religion of the Great Goddess* (San Francisco: Harper & Row, 1979), p. 9.
47. Karl Barth, *Church Dogmatics,* I, 1, (1936 & 1963), p. 447.
48. A book celebrating the revival of witchcraft as a feminist religion of the Goddess is Starhawk, *The Spiral Dance: A Rebirth of the Ancient Religion of the Great Goddess,* already cited in note 46. For a commendatory review of this book see Rosemary Ruether, "The Way of Wicca," *The Christian Century,* Vol. XCVII, No. 6 (February 20, 1980), pp. 208, 209. Ruether calls for a synthesis of "patriarchal historical religion and feminist nature religion."
49. Paul K. Jewett, *The Ordination of Women* (Grand Rapids: Eerdmans, 1980), pp. 44-47, 122, 127. I heartily concur with Jewett that it is indispensable to retain the personal language used by the Christian church in speaking of God. I also find myself in general basic agreement with Jewett in the case that he makes for women's ordination.
50. The God of Israel transcended the creaturely heavens as well as the earth (cf. 1 Kings 8:27; Ps. 57:5, 11; 108:5), and therefore the metaphor of "Sky Father" does not really do justice to the utter transcendence of the true God.

It is permissible as a metaphor but inadequate and even erroneous as an analogy. The symbol "Father-God," because it refers specifically to the God who reveals himself in Jesus Christ as heavenly Father, has a more literal connotation.

51. This does not mean that it is therefore permissible or proper to address deity in our public prayers by feminine as well as masculine imagery, though, as has been indicated, in certain contexts we may refer to the Word of God or the Wisdom of God as "Holy Mother" or "Heavenly Sister," since this has some biblical support. (In private devotions there could be more latitude in this area.) We may also refer to Christ as our "Elder Brother" (or something similar), since this, too, has a biblical basis (cf. Rom. 8:29; Col. 1:15; Matt. 28:10). In my opinion, references to the Spirit as "Mother" should generally (though not necessarily always) be restricted to the church as the historical bearer or vessel of the Spirit. Were it to become a general practice in our prayers to address God sometimes as "Father" and sometimes as "Mother," a case could be made that such a God would inevitably cease to be thought of as a personal being, and instead would come to be regarded as an impersonal or suprapersonal ground of being.

CHAPTER FIVE / *A Biblical Alternative*

1. Karl Barth, *Church Dogmatics,* III, 4, eds. G. W. Bromiley and T. F. Torrance (Edinburgh: T. & T. Clark, 1961), p. 123.
2. According to the Brahmin *Laws of Manu,* even when a husband gives himself to other women, the wife must do nothing to displease him.
3. Susan T. Foh, "Abortion and Women's Lib," in Richard L. Ganz, *Thou Shalt Not Kill* (New Rochelle, N.Y.: Arlington House Publishers, 1978), p. 171.
4. One can say that man and woman are created as souls infinitely and equally precious before God, but the way they are set in historical existence accounts for the fact that the feminine is subordinate to or dependent on the masculine.
5. John Howard Yoder rightly reminds us that all Christians are called to "revolutionary subordination," since the suffering of Jesus is the law of the life of his disciples. He contends that Paul did not borrow his subordinationist thought but instead created it by applying the central theme of Christology to a universal problem. The call to be subordinate or to regard another as higher than oneself "is addressed to men with regard to their wives and vice versa, slaves toward their masters (and again vice versa, compare Philemon), children toward their parents (and the parents should honour their children by not irritating them), the young toward the old, and the elders toward the congregation which they lead. . . . The subordinate person becomes a free ethical agent when he voluntarily accedes to his subordination in the power of Christ instead of bowing to it either fatalistically or resentfully." John H. Yoder, *The Politics of Jesus* (Grand Rapids: Eerdmans, 1972), pp. 163-192. The first quotation is Yoder's translation of a statement by Johannes Hamel.

6. Rosemary Ruether, "The Other Side of Marriage," *A.D.* Magazine, Vol. 8, No. 6 (June 1979), pp. 8, 9.
7. See the study document, *Language About God "Opening the Door,"* adopted by the 187th General Assembly of the United Presbyterian Church in the U.S.A. (New York: Advisory Council on Discipleship and Worship, 1975), p. 4.
8. For an incisive critique of feminism as a social ideology see Stephen Clark, *Man and Woman in Christ* (Ann Arbor, Mich.: Servant Books, 1980). Unfortunately Clark does not subject patriarchalism to the same kind of critical scrutiny.
9. Naomi Goldenberg, *Changing of the Gods* (Boston: Beacon Press, 1979), pp. 4, 10.
10. Women in the black and poor communities are reluctant to become involved in feminism, because the greatest need in their families is for the father to live up to his responsibility as a breadwinner and provider. Most poorer black families are in effect matriarchies, but the women generally do not want it this way. The conflict today between feminism and patriarchalism reflects the cleavage in our society between the old elite of the business and farming communities and the "new class"—intellectuals, educators, members of the "helping professions," and media people whose vested interests depend on state intervention. According to Peter Berger, the church must distance itself from both ideological currents so that it can be free to speak with a prophetic voice. See his "The Class Struggle in American Religion," *The Christian Century*, Vol. XCVIII, No. 6 (February 25, 1981), pp. 194-199.
11. Because a term like *mankind* still maintains a basically generic sense among the vast majority of people, my suggestion is that *humankind* or *humanity* be used as a supplement, but not as a substitute for it. It should be recognized that the term *mankind* preserves the biblical notion that woman has been taken from man and is included in man (cf. Gen. 2:21-23; 5:1, 2). A similar case could be made for the use of the generic *man*, though *man* preceded by either the definite or indefinite article now usually means specific, not generic man. Where words that were once generic tend to lose their generic meaning, there is a need for more inclusive language.
12. Harry Blamires, *Where Do We Stand?* (Ann Arbor, Mich.: Servant Books, 1980), p. 115.
13. "A Dialogue with Simone de Beauvoir" in Betty Friedan, *It Changed My Life: Writings on the Women's Movement* (New York: Random House, 1976), pp. 311, 312. Betty Friedan, who does not share this extreme view, makes clear her differences with the more radical feminism in her *The Second Stage* (New York: Summit Books, 1981).
14. Thomas Aquinas, *Summa Theologica,* I, 92, I, ad 2.
15. One strand in classical Calvinism creates the impression that one is automatically in the covenant community by virtue of being born of Christian parents. Calvin himself emphasized the need for personal faith and repentance, though he, too, was sometimes led into affirming that the children of parents in the covenant community were "presumably regenerate."

16. Billy Graham's assertion that "the appointed destiny of real womanhood" is to be "wife, mother, homemaker" is at best a half-truth of Scripture. Such a view concentrates only on certain biblical passages (such as Gen. 3:16 and Titus 2:4, 5) and ignores many others (including Luke 10:42; 11:27, 28; Matt. 27:55; 1 Cor. 7:8). See Billy Graham, "Jesus and the Liberated Woman," *Ladies' Home Journal,* Vol. 87, No. 12 (December 1970), p. 42.
17. Cf. Karl Barth: "Properly speaking, the business of woman, her task and function, is to actualise the fellowship in which man can only precede her, stimulating, leading, and inspiring. . . . To wish to replace him in this, or to do it with him, would be to wish not to be a woman." *Church Dogmatics,* III, 4, p. 171.
18. Another way to put this is that the Pauline meaning of subordination is a creative cooperation in which the man assumes a leadership role but with the aid and sanction of his wife, who functions as both his helpmate and critic. Exactly what this entails will differ for every couple, since gifts and talents are not always evenly distributed. It must always be remembered that the husband, too, is called to practice subordination (Eph. 5:21ff.); and if he rides roughshod over his wife's desires and interests, he is forfeiting his role as her *kephale.*
19. It is a fact that there are virtually no women included in the roster of the great philosophers either in the West or in the East. On the other hand, there are many women who have won renown as spiritual writers, poets, and novelists. Is this due to cultural conditioning, as feminists suppose, or may it be that women and men are endowed with different gifts and capabilities? This is not to imply that any particular gift or task is higher or more worthy than another.
20. Cited in Elisabeth Elliot, *Let Me Be a Woman* (Wheaton, Ill.: Tyndale House, 1976), p. 59.
21. Margaret Mead concludes on the basis of a crosscultural study of seven Pacific cultures that men and women differ in various areas of temperament and that these differences are rooted in biological realities. She believes that females are biologically predisposed to desire to bear and raise children, whereas males are characterized by restless ambition and a desire for achievement. Mead acknowledges that society can redirect these biological-psychological predispositions, but she nonetheless sees them as very significant. Margaret Mead, *Male and Female* (New York: William Morrow & Co., 1949). For an illuminating discussion of Margaret Mead's research as well as other anthropological and related social-scientific studies on male-female differences, see Stephen Clark, *Man and Woman in Christ,* pp. 371-448. Another significant study is that of Camilla Benbow, professor at Johns Hopkins University, who after eight years of research found that males have a higher aptitude for math than females and that the difference may be genetic. See *National Review,* Vol. XXXIII, No. 20 (Oct. 16, 1981), p. 1179. Such studies need to be taken with a certain degree of caution, but we must not close our eyes to the real possibility of genetic differences in this or other areas.

22. Karl Barth, *Church Dogmatics*, III, 4, p. 154. Barth sees the basic understanding of the masculine and feminine as grounded in revelation itself. His assessment is especially dependent on the Genesis account of the origin of humankind and also on Paul's depiction of Christian marriage as analogous to Christ's relationship to the church (Eph. 5:21ff); in this context, the church as the bride of Christ symbolizes the feminine.
23. Kate Millett, *Sexual Politics* (New York: Avon Books, 1970).
24. Romanticism has its roots in late medieval culture where knighthood and chivalry were held in high esteem. For the troubadour, who emerged in southern France and northern Italy in the eleventh and twelfth centuries, woman was no longer a sex object, but an object of adoration to whom he addressed poems from afar. For a brilliant treatment of the tensions between romanticism and Christian faith, see Sheldon Vanauken, *A Severe Mercy* (New York: Harper & Row, 1977).
25. In my reading of feminist literature, the emphasis is on husband and wife assisting each other in fulfilling separate careers rather than working together to realize a common vocation under the cross. Rivalry means trying to equal or outdo another, and it allows for cooperation as well as competition. Even though rivalry may not be intended in a marital relationship, it is virtually inevitable where the emphasis is on self-fulfillment in a career rather than on self-giving service to the forsaken and oppressed for whom Christ died.
26. That patriarchalism is still very much alive in Roman Catholicism is strikingly evident in the declaration of one Spanish language working group at the Synod of Bishops called by Pope John Paul II in October 1980: "Christian marriage must be considered as a vocation to fertility." *Time*, Vol. 116, No. 18 (November 3, 1980), p. 102.
27. Luther approached the covenantal model of marriage when he described marriage in the Lord as "a school of faith and love," since it calls for the constant exercise of sympathy, sacrifice, and patience. In other words, it has for one of its purposes training in Christian righteousness.
28. Barth's break with patriarchalism is evident in this statement of his: "Marriage is not subordinate to the family, but the family . . . to marriage. Marriage as life-partnership implies, of course, an inner readiness for children and therefore for the family to the extent that it is full sexual communion. But as a life-partnership it is in no way conditioned by the co-existence of children. It subsists even without the founding of a family, even as the life-partnership of a possibly childless marriage." *Church Dogmatics*, III, 4, p. 189.
29. For an able defense of celibacy in relationship to marriage by a Reformed theologian, see Max Thurian, *Marriage and Celibacy*, trans. Norma Emerton (London: SCM Press Ltd., 1959).
30. It is in this light that we can best understand Luther's statement in his *On Monastic Vows:* "Marriage is good, virginity is better, but liberty is best." Cited in Roland Bainton, *Here I Stand* (New York: Abingdon Press, 1950), p. 201.

31. I am thinking here of Kierkegaard's "teleological suspension of the ethical," in which the commandment of God takes precedence over moral obligations to our fellow human beings. If the call to kingdom-service should entail lengthy or even permanent separation from our spouse, our response must nevertheless be one of obedience to the divine imperative (cf. Luke 14:26). In such circumstances, however, one must be quite sure that one is serving God and not self.
32. Headship is no longer seen as domination but as tender care, just as subordination is now conceived as loving support rather than servile submission. Moderate feminism makes a place for mutual support in the marital relationship but not for the possible crucifixion of the man on behalf of his wife. Just as Christ was crucified for the sake of the church, so the husband must be willing to be crucified for the sake of his wife.
33. These comments on the moral situation in Sweden are based largely on Roland Huntford, *The New Totalitarians* (New York: Stein & Day, 1972); Robert Braun, *Was geht in Schweden eigentlich vor?* (Nürnberg: Glock and Lutz, 1967); Ami Lonnroth, "Current of Inequality That Runs Through Sweden's 'Feminist Utopia,' " *Des Moines Register* (March 19, 1980), p. 13/A; Tom G. A. Hardt, "Sweden's War on the Family," *Christianity Today*, Vol. XVI, No. 20 (July 7, 1972), pp. 36, 37; Deane William Ferm, "Is Swedish Sex For Us?", *Commonweal*, Vol. CVIII, No. 12 (June 19, 1981), pp. 363-366; and an interview with Alex Thompson of Campus Crusade for Christ, who with his wife is stationed in Gothenberg, Sweden; this interview took place at the Third Presbyterian Church in Dubuque, Iowa, August 17, 1979.
34. This is not to overlook the emergence of celibate religious orders and monastic houses in the Lutheran church of Sweden, but the number of applicants is thus far very small.
35. In a growing number of hospitals many babies are left to die after surviving abortion procedures. Two journalists report that "hundreds of times a year in the U.S., an aborted fetus emerges from the womb kicking and alive. This is what one medical expert on abortions calls 'the dreaded complication.' " Liz Jeffries and Rick Edmonds, "Live Abortion," *Des Moines Sunday Register* (August 30, 1981), pp. 1/E, 3/E. One witness testified that he actually saw one of these "doomed" babies deliberately killed after its birth. It is well to note that woman suffrage advocates in the nineteenth century generally opposed abortion, regarding it as "an undeserved punishment, and a woman who had one a helpless victim" of male selfishness. See Linda Gordon, "Voluntary Motherhood" in *Clio's Consciousness Raised*, Mary Hartman and Lois Banner, eds. (New York: Harper & Row, 1974), p. 63.
36. A restrictive patriarchalism is evident in varying degrees in evangelicals Bill Gothard and Marabel Morgan, though both also reflect some genuinely Christian concerns. Bill Gothard can be faulted for regarding the ancient Jewish family structure as the model for contemporary society. He sees the family structure in terms of a "chain of command" with the father as the ruling authority. For perceptive evangelical critiques of Bill Gothard's Insti-

tute in Basic Youth Conflicts see Frederick Wagner and William A. Dyrness, "Basic Youth Conflicts: A Closer Look" in *Eternity* Vol. 24, No. 11 (Nov. 1973), pp. 32-34, 50; and Joseph Bayly, "Basic Conflicts" and "How Basic the Conflict" in *Eternity*, Vol. 28, No. 6 (June 1977), pp. 60-62 and Vol. 28, No. 8 (August 1977), pp. 41-43. For a critical appraisal of Marabel Morgan's "Total Woman" from a biblical perspective, see Jeanne Kun, "A Woman of Strength, Who Can Find?" in *Pastoral Renewal*, Vol. 5, No. 8 (February 1981), pp. 61, 62. One can also discern elements of an authoritarian patriarchalism in Larry Christenson, *The Christian Family* (Minneapolis: Bethany Fellowship, 1970). For my criticisms of Christenson, see pp. 108, 109.

37. It can be argued that the love the husband is enjoined to give to his wife (Eph. 5:25) is much more demanding than the subordination required of the wife to her husband (Eph. 5:22), since love entails a sacrifice that goes beyond submission.

Scripture Index

Name Index

Subject Index